Preaching in the
New Creation

Preaching in the New Creation

The Promise of New Testament Apocalyptic Texts

DAVID SCHNASA JACOBSEN

Westminster John Knox Press
Louisville, Kentucky

Scripture quotations, unless otherwise noted, are from the New Revised Standard Version of the Bible, copyright © 1989 by the Division of Christian Education of the National Council of the Churches of Christ in the U.S.A., and are used by permission.

Scripture quotations from the Revised Standard Version of the Bible are copyright © 1946, 1952, 1971, and 1973 by the Division of Christian Education of the National Council of the Churches of Christ in the U.S.A. and are used by permission.

Excerpt from *Gespräche, Diskussionen, Aufsätze* copyright © 1969 by Ernestine Schlant and Irmgard Feix, and renewed 1997 by Irmgard Feix, reprinted by permission of Harcourt, Inc.

Book design by Sharon Adams
Cover design by Koechel Peterson & Associates

First edition
Published by Westminster John Knox Press
Louisville, Kentucky

This book is printed on acid-free paper that meets the American National Standards Institute Z39.48 standard. ♾

PRINTED IN THE UNITED STATES OF AMERICA
99 00 01 02 03 04 05 06 07 08 — 10 9 8 7 6 5 4 3 2 1

Library of Congress Cataloging-in-Publication Data
    Jacobsen, David Schnasa.
        Preaching in the new creation : the promise of New Testament apocalyptic texts / David Schnasa Jacobsen.
        p. cm.
        Includes bibliographical references and index.
        ISBN 0-664-25845-X (alk. paper)
        1. Apocalyptic literature.   2. Bible.   N.T.—Homiletical use.
    I. Title.
    BS646.J33   1999
    225'.046—dc21   99–30509

To Cindy, Christian, and Grace:
Your words make a world of difference to me.

Contents

Acknowledgments

For comments on the manuscript at various stages I wish to thank my wife, the Rev. Cindy Schnasa Jacobsen; my colleagues Profs. Harold Remus, Tim Hegedus, Bob Kelly; my editor, Dr. Carey Newman; Alannah Hegedus, who helped me with the final draft; and the Rev. Michael Rattee, an insightful and genial doctoral student in homiletics at the University of Toronto. In various ways, they have made this work better than it otherwise would have been.

Special appreciation also goes to all my other new friends and colleagues at Waterloo Lutheran Seminary (Wilfrid Laurier University) in Waterloo, Ontario, and in the Eastern Synod of the Evangelical Lutheran Church in Canada. I have been blessed by newfound conversation partners in the gospel. When we gather together for Word and Table, this United Methodist pastor experiences Christ's "real presence"!

There were of course others who helped bring this apocalyptic book to completion. Students in my course "Biblical Preaching: Apocalyptic Texts" always gave me a lot to think about. Their engaged creativity, theological depth, and commitment to justice helped convince me that this project was worth the effort. Kevin Powell, a fine M.Div. student and soon-to-be exceptional Lutheran pastor, was a big help as a research assistant. Erin Mitchell, a gifted graduate student in Religion and Culture, compiled the indexes. I also wish to gratefully acknowledge financial support for this research, a grant partly funded by Wilfrid Laurier University operating funds.

Thanks also go to friends who have encouraged me along the way: Prof. Ron Allen of Christian Theological Seminary in Indianapolis and Profs. David Buttrick and Susan Bond of Vanderbilt

Divinity School come especially to mind. In this project's early stages, they tested my thoughts and provoked new ones. I owe them all quite a debt.

Special thanks go to Dr. Richard Lischer of the Divinity School at Duke University, who helped chase down a troublesome quote. I also wish to express special thanks to Gary Kidwell, the editor of *Biblical Preaching Journal*. The sermons in Appendix 2 and some of the exegetical work sprinkled throughout the book first appeared in issues of his journal. Gary has graciously consented to their appearing here.

Finally, I wish to thank the churches I have pastored over the years: First United Methodist Church of Pierre, South Dakota; The Little Brown Church on the Prairie and Grace Lutheran in Hayes, South Dakota; and New Johnsonville First United Methodist Church in Tennessee. They endured my preaching with a steadfast patience of apocalyptic proportions. They have given me more than I can ever hope to repay.

Introduction

A New Angle of Vision

Imagine sitting in a church sanctuary looking at a stained-glass window of John's Holy City, the new Jerusalem. Filled with dazzling images from the Apocalypse, it offers an unusual vision. When looking through the new Jerusalem window, you see your own world in a different light: both as it is and as it might be. True, in the bright light of day, you might see outside to pot-holed roads, broken streetlights, and doors barred shut in fear. Yet, at the same time, you would also be looking out at that world through the images of John's fantastic apocalyptic vision. You see streets of gold, a gleam of radiant glory, and gates of pearl overlaying the frightened urban chaos. The stained-glass window's apocalyptic images actually function in two ways: bringing to light the brokenness and, yet, the possibility of your world.

This book arises out of the same dual vision. It presupposes that many apocalyptic texts in the New Testament have a similar revelatory potential for preaching. Although our churches often feel all too closed and our ecclesiastical futures far from open, apocalyptic texts, much like the stained-glass window of the new Jerusalem, afford preachers and congregations the opportunity to view ourselves and our world in a new way. Apocalyptic texts "bring out" features of our relationship to the world and put them in the light of the gospel. In fact, our sermons can be a place where Word and world meet, an occasion for announcing the new thing God is doing. Call it "preaching in the new creation."

Naturally, this requires an unusual approach to apocalyptic texts in the New Testament. For the longest time I was convinced that most if not all "apocalyptic" was bad. Sure, *prophetic* visions in the Hebrew Bible were good. After all, that kind of prophecy was this-worldly, historical, a "speaking for." "Apocalyptic," by contrast, was deficient because its visions were otherworldly, mythological, mere speculative prediction.

This book, however, invites preachers to suspend many assumptions about "apocalyptic" and to spend some time listening carefully to individual texts. This means, first of all, developing a road map for traveling through the odd world of these writings (chap. 1). Then we will pay attention to not just what apocalyptic texts said, but what their words are trying to do (chap. 2). Afterward, we will compare New Testament apocalyptic texts to others like them to see where they meet and/or undermine our expectations of these forms (chap. 3). Finally, it will mean considering how these texts offer a symbolic world to help us understand our world in a new light (chap. 4). A consideration of some sample passages from the lectionary in chapters 5–7 and sermons on some of those texts in Appendix 2 will demonstrate that some New Testament apocalyptic texts have many surprises in store. Rather than simply confirming what many of us have long felt about "apocalyptic," some apocalyptic texts can aid preachers in proclaiming the gospel by bringing Word and world back together, helping us in our work of "preaching in the new creation."

Many pastors harbor a healthy skepticism about preaching apocalyptic texts—and for good reasons. Some apocalyptic texts portray incredibly violent scenes (Rev. 6:7–8); others *seem* bent on promoting a kind of "raptured escapism" (1 Thess. 4:16–17), or worse, a feeling of vindictiveness among the faithful (Rev. 14:9–11; 20:11–15). Still others ascribe to God motives or actions at odds with God's revelation in the life, death, and resurrection of Jesus Christ (compare the sulfuric fate of the "cowardly" in Rev. 21:8 with Jesus' concern for the same in the Gospels).[1]

Combined with these theological concerns are also the technical problems of interpretation. For pastors today apocalyptic texts tend not to "reveal" (ἀποκαλύπτειν) so much as to conceal. The texts' unusual narrative forms and mythological cosmic symbols seem to resist interpretation.

The literary genre of John's Apocalypse offers a fine example for our consideration. Most preachers have a basic idea of how to read a Gospel or an epistle, because we still read biographies and letters today. Apocalypses, by contrast, use unfamiliar narrative forms. Although our contemporary culture evidences some fascination with apocalyptic ideas and literary motifs (predictions about the turn of the millennium, angels, or TV shows like

The X-Files), people today do not actually sit down at their desks to type out bona fide apocalypses on their computers. The genre "apocalypse" is just not a normal way of communicating in our everyday world.

Similar problems show up when preachers attempt to deal with apocalyptic images such as earthquakes or angelic armies. Although the pulpit can hardly plumb all the mysteries of familiar symbols like the cross, water, wine, or bread, at least preachers have some things to say about them. We often invoke such symbols in our sermons. By contrast, apocalyptic symbols—blood-red moons, careening stars, multihorned beasts—seem to point to realities outside our experience and leave us speechless.

Nonetheless, there are good reasons for getting over our reluctance to deal with apocalyptic texts. In the end, we who are charged with preaching the gospel in this time and place cannot remain speechless about them.

First, we who preach are faced with tragic pastoral situations as the millennia turn. Already many groups responding to literalistic interpretations of such texts have played out apocalyptic timetables with deadly results. Recent tragedies like those of the Branch Davidians should give us pause. Rather than passing over apocalyptic texts in silence, perhaps we can deal with them more openly and honestly.

Second, fringe groups are not the only persons troubled by apocalyptic texts. Our culture's use of these texts to perpetuate apocalyptic fear and hype impacts many people in parishes today, too. The headlines of the tabloids staring at us as we stand in the supermarket checkout line or a TV preacher's end-time declamations rightly rouse our pastoral concern. Many of our contemporaries are using literalistic readings of texts like John's Apocalypse in a way that causes great anxiety among some and a vague dis-ease among others. We may want to preach these texts out of pastoral concern for the broader effects of apocalyptic *mis*-interpretation on our parishioners and the world in which we live.

Yet preaching these problematic texts is not just another onerous pastoral obligation. Rather, it is quite possibly a homiletical opportunity. Indeed, apocalyptic texts can offer a powerful vision of a more liberating social world.

Over the past twenty years not a few biblical commentators and church leaders have caught sight of the liberating vision of some apocalyptic texts. North American biblical scholar Elisabeth Schüssler Fiorenza views Revelation as supporting a praxis of consistent resistance by offering an alternative vision, a different way of reading the world, that emboldens the oppressed in the struggle for justice.[2] Pablo Richard, a Chilean priest and theologian living in Costa Rica, has developed a "people's commentary" on Revelation which brings together reflections of the poor in "base communities" and the conversations of international scholars who study John's Apocalypse. Richard writes: "Revelation transmits a spirituality of resistance and offers guidance for organizing an alternative world."[3] A decade ago, South African church leader Allan Boesak published Bible studies and sermons on the Apocalypse. His book, *Comfort and Protest,* read Revelation in order to strengthen people who were struggling against Apartheid.[4] These books represent just a sampling. In many corners of the world, Christians longing for liberation are recognizing the power of apocalyptic literature for keeping faith in the struggle.

The question then becomes: What about us? How can these texts become liberating for us, whose lives are usually more privileged than oppressed? The answer will require a different approach to interpreting these texts, one that takes seriously the problems they pose for preachers of the gospel. Although there may be times when we as preachers will rightly dismiss some aspect of apocalyptic texts for due cause (for example, the manifest misogyny of the Jezebel material in Rev. 2:20–22), we must also learn to be open to the surprising Word they offer us. Indeed, given our cultural context, perhaps we need to turn the question around. Instead of asking, "How do *we* interpret apocalyptic texts?" maybe we should ponder whether they are already interpreting *us.*

THE END OF OUR "SOCIAL" WORLD

Imagine you are sitting in a pastor's study in a creaky, old church, one of those dark-bricked Akron models. It is time to prepare your sermon and you find yourself staring out the window. Outside you see the last remnants of autumn leaves circling in a dreary brown drab across the dormant lawn. Why do you while away your precious sermon preparation time? Because it is the twenty-somethingth week after Pentecost—and your job is to preach the gospel with some apocalyptic lectionary text.

For a while preaching during Ordinary Time had looked attractive. During the summer and into the early fall there were engaging parable lections, some nice semi-continuous readings from Hebrew Bible narratives, and an occasional epistle text that just begged to be preached.

Yet the warm days of summer are now gone. They have given way to the winding down of the season after Pentecost. Now for a few weeks the lectionary fare will look less than satisfying: a month's worth of apocalyptic bombast for the rest of November and the beginning of Advent, too. It may just be enough to make a devoted lectionary preacher go topical!

These texts seem to hold little gospel, make precious few connections, and offer no relevance to us in our world. When it comes to apocalyptic texts, our first impulse may be to pass by in silence.

The problem is that some people are more than happy to talk about the apocalyptic texts haunting our lectionaries. In all likelihood, your parishioners are as skeptical as you are about millennial fear mongering. Yet they are also aware that their world is not as stable as it used to be. Perhaps, like you, they stare out their windows at rain-dark branches and swirling vestiges of leaves. Maybe, like you holed away in your study, they are also aware of endings: the end of a world where you could count on a stable job or where you could expect the church had an established role in the community. Now that "social" world seems just so far away. So many of your parishioners do not even live close to their church any more. They have moved to the homogenized suburbs where they can cocoon away in middle-class privacy. As for the ones who stayed behind, they hide behind iron bars on their windows, or else put up tiny security company signs on their postage-stamp lawns to give the illusion that they are protected from chaos. Our parishioners may not be full-blown, end-of-the-world, wild-eyed apocalyptic literalists, but they are painfully aware that something of their "social world" is passing away.

Perhaps, then, the end-of-the-world rhetoric of apocalyptic literature is not just some "thing" we try to interpret; it is in fact already interpreting our world. Maybe we have been deluding ourselves, sitting there brooding in our studies. We are not faced with a stable Word in a stable institution set in a stable world. In fact, the cosmic chaos of apocalypses helps to "bring out" important features of how we experience our lives in the world, their lived "instability." Now all the experiences of breakdown and social change rush back to awareness. It is not just our churches that are creaking and groaning in the last stages of death; it is our "social world."

Even this, though, is just a piece of the truth. It is not enough to recognize that apocalypses help us to see the instability of our world. It is equally true that they bring out the deepest and darkest of our fears. We are not just losing the world that we know; we *fear* losing it. Perhaps that is why so many of the scientific objections that we make about apocalyptic texts have never quite resolved the problem for us. Literalistic, apocalyptic thinking strikes us as implausible.

Yet, if these texts still do challenge our awareness, perhaps it is for reasons other than scientific reservations, namely, political reasons. Many contemporary interpreters argue that John's Apocalypse is not the product of a first-century fundamentalist, but is actually a vision for liberation. Indeed, perhaps it is the same kind of cosmic vision that Martin Luther King Jr. caught in his immortal words: "The arc of the moral universe is long, but it bends toward justice."[5]

Then maybe there is a liberating word for us, too. To be sure, it will not have the same impact as for those who wonder where their next meal is coming from. But there is a part of us that longs for change—even if it costs us something. We are, collectively, the chief beneficiaries of the global economy. The problem is that we have also made ourselves the world's taskmasters—given the bloody tracks of history, a pretty lousy position to have in the long run. Perhaps that is why we find ourselves worrying about what the "help" is up to: terrorism, currency devaluations, overseas market crashes. It kind of makes one wonder about the men who cracked the whips for Pharaoh before the exodus. Did they sleep well at night knowing that the people they oppressed had little to lose? Enough sleepless nights of our own might nudge even people like us into trading in old visions for new. In a world where Adam Smith's invisible hand promised but has never delivered "the wealth of nations," is there not a place for a vision where nobody need go thirsty (Rev. 21:6), a vision of tears wiped away (Rev. 21:4), a vision of a tree whose leaves are for healing the nations (Rev. 22:2)?[6] You remember: *a vision like the one in the stained-glass window of the new Jerusalem*—a vision that draws our eyes not inside, but outside the church to the new creation God has begun through Christ. Now that would be a gift worth receiving—a good enough gift to help us relinquish our old world of privilege.

So the liberating Word of apocalyptic texts may just be for us, too. True, for us, they approach as both promise and threat. Yet as we in the churches see our old social world slipping away, we may also discover something grace-full about relinquishing our privilege. Indeed, we may actually speak the gospel again as we try "preaching in the new creation."

---

1. "The one seated on the throne" in Rev. 21:8 reacts quite differently to the cowardly (δειλοῖς) than Jesus does to them (δειλοί) in Matt. 8:26!
2. Elisabeth Schüssler Fiorenza, *Revelation: Vision of a Just World* (Minneapolis: Fortress, 1991).
3. Pablo Richard, *Apocalypse* (Maryknoll, N.Y.: Orbis, 1995), 3.
4. Allan A. Boesak, *Comfort and Protest: Reflections on the Apocalypse of John of Patmos* (Philadelphia: Westminster, 1987).
5. Martin Luther King Jr., "Our God Is Marching On," in *A Testament of Hope,* ed. James M. Washington (San Francisco: Harper, 1986), 230. The use of the word "arm" for "arc" in this text is apparently a misprint.
6. Adam Smith, *The Wealth of Nations* (Toronto: Random House, 1937), 437.

Chapter 1

A Road Map for an Odd World

In the movie *The Wizard of Oz,* a powerful Kansas twister tosses Dorothy and her little dog Toto into an odd, technicolor world of strange beings and an emerald city. Looking around, Dorothy and Toto were no doubt disoriented about where they were and what they were facing. Whatever this strange land of Oz was, it certainly was not home. Oz was no Kansas!

Preachers daring to try to preach an apocalyptic text from the New Testament may feel the same way. Little about apocalyptic texts feels familiar. They are anywhere but "Kansas." So given our lack of familiarity, we need all the more to proceed with some kind of road map through the surprising world of apocalyptic texts. Dorothy and Toto had the typically Hollywood good fortune of a yellow-brick road to follow. We, however, will need to be more deliberate and circumspect as we go. We will require clarity about our *destination,* our *route,* and the meaning of the *signs* we see along the way.

The three methods we will use in the following chapters are not chosen willy-nilly. They are designed to help us navigate the odd world of apocalyptic texts in such a way that we have something to talk about on Sunday morning. In other words, they provide us with a road map that can help us prepare to preach.

Thus, insofar as we consider the rhetoric of apocalypses and apocalyptic texts, we will arrive at some sense of what our sermons can *do*. In other words, what apocalyptic texts *do* will provide us with a destination for our sermonic journeys.

Paying attention to the *form* of an apocalyptic text is important for showing us how we get there, the homiletical route we will take. Here, an analysis of apocalyptic forms will help us figure out how to structure our sermons toward our destinations.

With our analysis of cosmic, apocalyptic images, we will bring into clearer focus *the odd symbolic world of apocalypses*. This method will serve as a means of clarifying its signs. This way, the journey can be meaningful for our hearers, too.

THE RIGHT MAP FOR THE TRIP

The problem with maps, however, is that they are only good for certain purposes. Chances are, a geologist's map of all the caves in New Mexico will do you little good if you need to drive a car from Los Alamos to Santa Fe. Since our road map is designed for a homiletical purpose, it focuses on certain elements of the textual topography. Our road map foregrounds not so much the world "behind" an apocalyptic text but the world "in front" of it.[1]

Traditionally, biblical scholarship, especially the classic, historical-critical variety, has been interested in the world behind the text. Scholars of apocalyptic texts have tended to ask, "What kind of historical context could have produced texts as odd as apocalypses?"[2] Their research and findings have been influential in the study of apocalyptic texts.

Yet the world behind the text will not be our exegetical focus. Our road map will rarely cover that ground! Rather, we will look at the world in front of the text. Such a perspective focuses not so much on the context that produced apocalyptic literature as on the ways in which apocalypses *alter* a given context for hearers. In other words, we will not simply assume that apocalypses reflect their world; we will look at how they try to change it.[3]

By doing so, however, I am also inviting you to join me in yet another aspect of travel with a road map: the lover's quarrel. Traveling with loved ones can produce spats over the route, the destination, or even where to turn next. Our journey may occasion the same sort of spats. In the course of my studies, I have enjoyed getting to know the great traditions of modern biblical scholarship. In fact, I love the field of biblical studies almost as much as my own chosen discipline, homiletics. Therefore, when I take issue with ways in which we tend to fixate on the world behind the text, I do so not as an enemy of classical biblical criticism but as an ardent admirer. As often as I attempt to modify some of the typical ways we preachers have used the historical-critical approach to scripture, I do so as one who is convinced that critical engagement with biblical texts is indispensable and that historical criticism needs to be part (though not all) of the panoply of methods available to the homiletical exegete. Any harsh words that follow, therefore, should be understood in the context of my lover's quarrel with the way in which historical criticism has dominated biblical studies in the minds of those who interpret texts for preaching.

What is the nature of the spat? From the standpoint of preaching, historical criticism has been both a homiletical blessing and a curse. Broadly, its influence has helped shape what we might call preachers' modern "historical consciousness." The notion as I am describing it can be summed up in a simple phrase with which we instinctively recognize the distance between the history behind biblical texts and ourselves: "that was then, this is now."[4] To be sure, an awareness of the gap between ancient and modern worlds is important for understanding biblical texts critically. Yet this gain has not come without loss.

For some preachers, the gap between the biblical text and our context has led them to dismiss in the name of relevance what historically minded interpreters have found. Some may even assume that biblical criticism is more of a hindrance than a help to their task. Preachers who have embraced historical understanding, however, have experienced different problems. For many, historical awareness has contributed to contortions in the language of preaching, as we will see below. Suffice it to say, it is not easy to span two thousand years in a single sermon when the task is to preach the gospel to flesh-and-blood people seated in the pews.

Historical criticism has often been practiced in such a way that it has begotten interpretive claims for historical understanding that go beyond the mere application of a method. In other words, the very important and necessary practice of historical study has led to the unfortunate conclusion that historical context is the *only* critically viable way to engage biblical texts. I call this unintended result of historical criticism in exegesis and preaching the hermeneutical priority of historical understanding.[5] Again, there is no doubt that a general orientation to biblical texts as history has freed us from inappropriate (frequently overly dogmatic) readings of biblical texts. Yet for all its benefits, historical consciousness and the hermeneutical priority of historical understanding have bequeathed some unique problems for exegetes who interpret for preaching.

First, we tend to treat texts mostly as objects of critical study, that is, as primarily historical artifacts. This objectifying method was designed to restrain *eisegesis,* or reading into a passage our own projections and prejudices. Yet, as necessary as it is, this historical objectification also made it hard for us to think of biblical texts as anything but objects in our preaching.[6]

Second, historical criticism tended to view these objectified texts as the products of historical processes. In the name of locating a pericope's historical context (a laudable goal), it tended to assume that the best way to understand it was to see it as the result of various prior historical forces. In other words, a passage is first and foremost an "expression" of its historical context.

Third, historical criticism's tendency to beget a tacit hermeneutical priority for history led us preachers to assume that whatever the truth of a text was, it needed to be found in its origin. Contemporary meaning was fine, although such meaning was limited to being an extrapolation from the original truth arrived at by the historian (*wie es eigentlich gewesen*).[7] For real truth, we must read the past. Contemporary meaning is only a derivative meaning—derived, that is, from an authoritative, originating Truth.

Of course, the rise of historical criticism, our historical consciousness, and its hermeneutical priority is no small achievement. The beauty of the historical approach is that it helped authorize a critical way of approaching biblical texts. We could, in other words, ask questions of passages and be open to their answers—not simply assume or pretend to know what they said on the basis of our preconceptions. This contribution must not be underestimated.

Yet the problem for we who would proclaim the gospel with the aid of apocalyptic texts is how historical consciousness has not only blessed but also contorted our preaching and our relationship to the Bible. In many ways, our historical consciousness contributes to the uniquely Western way that our minds split between past and present, subject and object, ancient Truth and contemporary derivation of meaning. But the problem is not just one of dry intellectual history. Our congregations hear it in our sermons in the peculiar ways in which we sometimes talk. For example, in our words there is often a past/present split that cavalierly inserts the passing of several millennia between one sentence and the next:

> Of course we must remember that in Abraham's day, polygamy was a viable option. Now turn and consider our world: today, by contrast, serial monogamy is more the norm . . .

Or there is the standard objectifying line that asks listeners in the pew to pay attention to our spoken words while imagining themselves actually viewing columns of a text on a page:

God loves us with an all-consuming love—a love that does not know the limitations of our human loves. How do we know God loves us so? As we see in our text for today . . .

Or there is the problem with applying a text whose historical context is so different from ours as to make any homiletical use comical:

Therefore we can say with some surety that the Canaanites practiced their fertility cult within the institution of sacred prostitution, which celebrated the productive union between Baal and Asherah.

So what do the Canaanites have to do with us today? Well, deep down, friends, there is a little Canaanite in all of us . . .

From the caricatured examples above we may be able to begin discerning our problem. When interpreting the Bible, our desire to be historically minded—a worthy goal—may just be distorting the language of proclamation. Yet our historical minds' splits between past and present, subject and object, and ancient Truth and derivative application have often left us tongue-tied. The result is that we sometimes end up talking about texts as if sermons were book reports, rather than addressing people *through* texts as a means of proclaiming the gospel.

It is important to realize that historical criticism has enhanced preaching in many ways. We are heirs of a rich historical heritage. Our preaching has benefited from historians' work, and doubtless so have our hearers.

Yet for the sake of the gospel and those who sit in the pews before us week after week, we should stretch biblical interpretation beyond a purely historical conception of its work. In this book we will do just that. The chapters on apocalyptic rhetoric (chap. 2), form (chap. 3), and symbol (chap. 4) will focus less on the world behind the text and more on the world offered before it. This does not mean all historical questions are out of bounds—far from it. Rather, it means historical understanding will be put at the service of a critical engagement with: what *destination* a text intends, the *route* it takes to get there, and the *signs* it offers along the way.

EVERY ROAD MAP NEEDS A KEY

Of course, road maps do not do a whole lot of good if you cannot decipher what is, say, an expressway, and what is a dirt road. That is why most road maps provide, typically in one of the corners, an explanation of the road signs and symbols in a key or legend. In navigating the world of apocalypses we will also need a key to make the going easier. Since many of us assume that the words "apocalyptic" and "apocalypses" are interchangeable, it is important to be clear how to use terms. In other words, an apocalyptic road map needs a key, too.

The problem of defining terms is posed also by the texts themselves. There is, after all, only one example of the apocalyptic genre in the New Testament: namely, Revelation. Whatever the genres of the other New Testament writings are, they are certainly not apocalypses. Nonetheless, we sense when reading biblical texts that apocalyptic material keeps showing up elsewhere: sometimes in Gospels (Mark 13; Matthew 24; Luke 21), sometimes in letters (1 Thess. 4:13–18). While it might be possible to group the sections in the New Testament where apocalyptic motifs show up under the adjectival heading "apocalyptic," this unattached, adjectival term seems too imprecise. "Apocalyptic *what*?" we might wish to ask.

Thus, in order to consider the relationships between these different New Testament texts and to stick to some usable definition of terms, we will follow Paul D. Hanson's terminological distinctions. Hanson argues that it is useful to distinguish three particular aspects of what we often call, rather imprecisely, "apocalyptic." Apocalypse refers to the literary genre; apocalypticism, to the social phenomenon; and apocalyptic eschatology, to its unique way of viewing the future.[8] While Hanson's distinctions are not perfect, we can take one important cue from him.[9] Since part of our concern focuses on how apocalyptic forms get used in texts that are *not* apocalypses, we should carefully distinguish between apocalypses (the literary genre) and the use of apocalyptic literary motifs in other genres. In the chapters to follow, therefore, we will not use the term "apocalyptic" unless it is attached to some other noun. Thus, for the most part the adjective "apocalyptic" will stand next to literary terms such as "motif," "text," or "type scene."

The question then arises: What consititutes an apocalypse? In this book we will rely on the definition first developed in 1979 by the Apocalypse Group of the Society of Biblical Literature Genres Project and supplemented in 1986:

> Apocalypse is a genre of revelatory literature with a narrative framework, in which a revelation is mediated by an otherworldly being to a human recipient, disclosing a transcendent reality which is both temporal, insofar as it envisages eschatological salvation, and spatial insofar as it involves another, supernatural world intended to interpret present, earthly circumstances in light of the supernatural world and of the future, and to influence both the understanding and the behavior of the audience by means of divine authority.[10]

This definition has many advantages. Above all, it describes the apocalypse in largely literary terms. The definition remains free of historical and sociological determinants (the world *behind the text*) and thus helpfully maintains the distinctions between literary and sociological or historical apocalyptic phenomena. This definition also comes with the Apocalypse Group's careful feature-by-feature description of several apocalyptic texts, some of which are designated apocalypses (for example, Jewish, Christian) and others of which are viewed as "related types."[11] Their description will provide us with a useful literary baseline for comparing texts that are apocalypses and texts that share some different kind of literary relationship with the genre.

CAUTION: ROAD HAZARDS

Before leaving on our trip through apocalyptic texts, it is good to make note of what we can anticipate along the way. A good road map highlights both desired destinations and the hazards a traveler might face.

Learning a new way of interpreting biblical texts is a great way to see new vistas. There is nothing like the exhilaration of finding something new in a text. At that moment, you realize that rather than just having a sermon, a sermon has you. Those moments make all the hard work of wrestling seem worth it—even if at the time it felt like sweat and desperation.

However, learning new ways of interpreting apocalyptic texts often means driving some difficult stretches *before* we reach our dream destination. Interpreting apocalyptic texts step-by-step will at first feel awkward. Part of it is the difficulty of doing things in a new way. Part of it is also dealing with detours, realizing that every text is unique and may mean adjusting an interpretive approach. The key is to trust that even detours eventually take you home and that the awkwardness in time yields to grace. Then the map is no longer a distraction from the journey, nor does it take the place of the trip. Instead, it becomes what it was always meant to be: a means of finding your way to what you've never seen before.

The three methods that I am offering in the following chapters are intended to be useful for preachers in precisely this way. They are just means of navigating those apocalyptic lections that don't readily yield up the form of a sermon. For those readers who come to this text for reasons other than mastering new methods, however, a road hazard should be marked. Chapter 5 may prove to be the toughest stretch to travel. You may wish to skim this chapter if that is what it takes to arrive intact at the end of the book. Journeys are rarely satisfying when you find that you can't navigate the terrain and give up on the trip. Let it be said, however, that road trips, even arduous ones, hold surprising vistas in store for those who go the distance.

So, with our road map in hand, we can now begin to find our way in the odd world of apocalyptic texts. True, the landscape through which we travel may not look quite like "Kansas." Yet as we go, we may just find something more than the familiar: a way to "preach in the new creation."

---

1. The distinction between the worlds "behind" and "in front of" the text comes from Paul Ricoeur (*Interpretation Theory: Discourse and the Surplus of Meaning* [Fort Worth: Texas Christian Univ. Press, 1976], 87). The distinction has been further elaborated by many who wish to expand the methodological options and hermeneutical priority of the historical-critical approach to exegesis. Edgar McKnight offers a very readable autobiographical account of how this sea change in biblical criticism figured into his own critical development (*The Bible and the Reader: An Introduction to Literary Criticism* [Philadelphia: Fortress, 1985], xi–xix, esp. xviii). Sandra Schneiders has put Ricoeur's distinction to use in her attempt to locate multiple methodological options, including historical-critical ones, into an integrated, theological approach to biblical hermeneutics (*The Revelatory Text: Interpreting the New Testament as Sacred Scripture* [New York: HarperCollins, 1991]).

2. New Testament literary critic Norman Petersen has described this move as a genetic understanding of the practice of historical criticism in biblical studies (*Literary Criticism for New Testament Critics* [Philadelphia: Fortress, 1978], 25–26). The tendency in the history of classical, historical-critical scholarship to find a unified origin, genesis, or single social setting of apocalyptic texts has been noted most recently in the work of John J. Collins (*The Apocalyptic Imagination,* 2d ed. [Grand Rapids: Eerdmans, 1998], 37–38).

3. Sandra Schneiders may be describing something similar when she talks about the difference between reading for "information" and "transformation" (*Revelatory Text,* 13–14). Edgar McKnight views historical-criticism's tendency to offer "genetic" readings of biblical texts as problematic given the reader's partnership in making meaning (*Postmodern Use of the Bible: The Emergence of Reader-Oriented Criticism* [Nashville: Abingdon, 1988], 67–114). William Beardslee is concerned that in the search for historical causes, critics run the risk of turning away from the text itself (*Literary Criticism of the New Testament* [Philadelphia: Fortress, 1969], 6f.). In every case, however, the danger is seen in reducing the text to little more than an effect of historical causes.

4. There is an irony to this split in contemporary awareness. On the one hand historical critics of the Bible, like Edgar Krentz, can celebrate the fact that the method has clearly distinguished the ancient world from our own as a means of preventing a kind of dogmatic or pietistic *eisegesis* and collapse of past into present (*The Historical-Critical Method* [Philadelphia: Fortress, 1975], 64–65). On the other hand, they also take pains to demonstrate that historical criticism, following Troeltsch's essay "On Historical and Dogmatic Method in Theology," proceeds on the assumption of an *analogy* between present and past, namely, "that all events are in principle similar" (Krentz, *Historical-Critical Method,* 87; compare Van Harvey, *The Historian and the Believer* [Philadelphia: Westminster, 1966], 14ff.). From my perspective, historical criticism has succeeded in

inculcating the former rather than the latter in contemporary exegesis and preaching.

5. Many of the recent attempts to recast the role of historical criticism in the work of biblical exegesis have done so with a view not to eliminating its influence, but to setting it alongside a variety of methodological options—especially literary (Beardslee, *Literary Criticism,* 7; McKnight, *Postmodern,* 67; Petersen, *Literary Criticism for New Testament Critics,* 24–33), sociological (Howard Clark Kee, *Knowing the Truth: A Sociological Approach to New Testament Interpretation* [Minneapolis: Fortress, 1989], 22–26), and even theological/spiritual (Schneiders, *Revelatory Text,* 22–25).

6. In actuality, any critical method, not just historical criticism, objectifies a text as a critical moment in the process of coming to understanding. The question is whether a text must remain an object when a preacher begins the task of proclamation.

7. The phrase was made popular by the work of the classic German historian von Ranke.

8. Paul D. Hanson, "Apocalypticism," in *Interpreter's Dictionary of the Bible Supplementary Volume,* ed. Keith Crim (Nashville: Abingdon, 1976), 29–31.

9. Michael Stone notes that we frequently overemphasize eschatology at the expense of other dimensions, e.g., speculative knowledge ("Lists of Revealed Things in the Apocalyptic Literature," in *Magnalia Dei: The Mighty Acts of God: Essays on the Bible and Archaeology in Memory of G. Ernest Wright,* ed. Frank M. Cross, William Lemke, and Patrick Miller [Garden City, N.Y.: Doubleday, 1976], 443).

10. Adela Yarbro Collins, "Early Christian Apocalypticism: Genre and Social Setting," *Semeia* 36 (1986): 2, 7.

11. John J. Collins, "Introduction: Towards the Morphology of a Genre," *Semeia* 14 (1979): 18.

Chapter 2

Where in the World We Are Going:
What Apocalyptic Texts Do

Apocalyptic texts are populated by angelic armies, dragons, death-dealing pale riders, and throngs of white-robed martyrs. We experience them as oddly distant and dated, the product of a bygone worldview. For the most part, apocalyptic texts leave us contemporary preachers scratching our heads.

However, what if the problem is not the texts themselves but the way we typically look at them? Most of us probably cut our exegetical teeth on the classic historical-critical method. In part supported by a biblical theology focusing on separating (*a*) what the text meant in its context and (*b*) what the text means in ours, we have tended to treat texts as distanced *objects* of critical study, that is, as products of an ancient context, or historical artifacts.[1] What if, however, we could view our texts as not only arising out of historical situations, but trying to shape them? Moreover, what if their truth were not static, given objects, but dynamic events between speakers and hearers?[2] Perhaps our exegesis would look quite different if we focused not just on what texts once said but on what they *do*.

To illustrate, let's say someone in a crowded movie theater smells smoke. Startled by this olfactory intrusion on her moviegoing experience, she glances at the lower right corner of the retracted velvet curtain in front. Because the other moviegoers' eyes are fixed on the screen, she is the only one who sees fire beginning to lick the velvet curtain's bottom edge. Instinctively, she shouts out, "Fire!" What do you suppose the other moviegoers' reaction to her one-word proclamation would be? Certainly it would be absurd for them to gather in discussion groups considering the history of the word "fire" in Indo-European languages between the now toasty-warm rows of sticky theater seats. Likewise, it would be bizarre to convene an on-the-spot physics seminar about the thermodynamics of combustion as the aisles fill up with smoke. We know, almost instinctively, that when someone yells "Fire" in a crowded theater, the word does not function solely to describe something "out there." It has, rather, a more compelling rhetorical purpose. This is to say that yelling "Fire" in a cinema is not just about expressing something, it is about *doing* something, as in, "Get out of this theater!"[3]

Such an approach to language can help us in interpreting apocalyptic texts for preaching. We have often assumed that a rational, objectivist, and ultimately historicist understanding of the Bible could tell us the exhaustive truth about texts.[4] Yet if we assume such an approach, no wonder apocalyptic texts seem beyond the pale! Any rational, objective person would have to conclude that apocalyptic texts are either (*a*) patently false, (*b*) primitively supernaturalistic, or (*c*) the product of a deluded mind. However, if apocalyptic texts are understood not just for what they once said but for what they intend to *do,* namely, how they function rhetorically, then we can begin to make sense of them and imagine how they might *do* something in our own homiletical contexts.

Of course, such an understanding of language is not altogether new. In everyday reality we distinguish intuitively between what words say and what they do. When we hear a friend tell a joke or a parent recite a bedtime fairy tale or a friend relate the plot of a science fiction TV show, the last thing they'd expect from us is a question about whether the joke, fairy tale, or TV show really happened! Most of the time, jokes intend laughter; fairy tales, sleep; and science fiction shows, reflective futuring. In fact, if we were so pedantic about objective historical truth, we would in all likelihood lose friends, alienate our parents, and keep our eyes glued to the History Channel and never watch the news. In other words, we just seem to know that language is not solely about objective things, but also intends to do something in relation to hearers today.

The question then arises: What in the world are apocalyptic biblical texts doing? Assuming for a moment that what they do can help us figure out what to do when we preach them, how can we find it out? The shift from more static, objectivist, and historically oriented understandings of exegesis to more dynamic, relational ones may just be the key. Yet the question of exegetical method is actually grounded on a more fundamental one: the homiletical and theological question of what we are looking for when we interpret a text.

BEYOND HOMILETICAL OBJECTIVISM

We must acknowledge the sea change in homiletics that has allowed us even to pose the question we do. There is a parallel between the important shifts in biblical criticism and in homiletic theory relative to the sureties of historical knowledge and the science of truth.

In 1969 a tantalizing little book by David Randolph, *The Renewal of Preaching,* began to draw connections between the "new hermeneutic" of Bultmann's students and an emerging "new homiletic."[5] Although Randolph's book only begins to draw the broadest outlines of what will develop later, it seems to represent a dawning of an approach that doesn't view the biblical text as a thing, but, in the language of the new hermeneutic, as a "word event." Already, it was becoming possible to think of a homiletic method that focuses on texts not so much as static, dead repositories of ancient truth, but as occasions for preaching a living, doing Word.

With Fred Craddock's landmark work, *As One without Authority,* the notion began to be pushed even further. Among other things, Craddock suggested that the form of the text might produce a variety of sermon forms.[6] In his own way Craddock was considering the way in which the language events of text and sermon were the means by which Word happened. Indeed for Craddock, the "how" of the sermon's movement was just as important as the "what" that was being preached.

Since then, many homileticians have articulated various ways of approaching biblical texts for preaching. Narrative homileticians have pinned their work not just to what the text says but to what it does by focusing on the narrative shape of scripture or the narrative shape of the sermon itself.[7] Still others consider what scripture texts do relative to human consciousness and/or contemporary sermon forms themselves.[8] Much of what has passed for new in the so-called new homiletic has focused on matters of what texts and sermons *do.*

A Brief Theology of the Word That Does

Yet the desire to move past objectivist understandings of exegesis and preaching must go beyond merely aping the latest homiletical trends. Indeed, if preaching does not have some sort of theological moorings, it runs the risk of being merely faddish. Therefore, if we are to venture boldly into preaching by means of what apocalyptic texts do and not just what they once said, we must lay at least a little theological groundwork for doing so.

First, any decent theology of the Word must acknowledge that that self-same Word is not a thing, but a happening: a Word-event. Of course, the scriptures themselves have long witnessed to the dynamism of the divine Word. At creation, God speaks the Word and the world comes to pass (Gen. 1:3–27). The prophet Isaiah attests to the power of the divine Word not to "return empty" (Isa. 55:11). For the writer of Hebrews, the Word is "sharper than any two-edged sword" (Heb. 4:12). Often the scriptures, the very texts we tend to objectify, point not to themselves as a repository of static truth but to the efficacious, dynamic truth of the divine Word in action.

For we who call ourselves by Christ's name, that Word has received special form in the life, death, and resurrection of Jesus. Indeed, the significance of Christ as Word has been not only claimed for Jesus' life in history but located in the first stirrings of creation and the ultimate closure of consummation. "Through him all things were made," we say in the words of the Nicene Creed, and "and he will come again in glory." Tellingly, some biblical witnesses have already grasped this far-reaching dynamism of the divine Word ahead of the Council of Nicaea. In John's prologue, the Word is seen as being creatively present with God "in the beginning" (John 1). The writer of the letter to the Colossians also noted the Word's activity in Christ from creation on (Col. 1:15–16). However, creation is not the only place where the Bible envisions the Word "doing." Scripture also points toward Christ's role in the consummation of all things, defeating God's adversaries precisely as "The Word of God" (Rev. 19:11–16). Similarly, Paul can say in the mythic language of eschatology that the same Christ, who was revealed in the self-giving of the cross, will in the end hand over the kingdom to God so that God may be all in all (1 Cor. 15:24–28). With some frequency, the scriptures themselves talk about the Word not as a static truth but as an ongoing creative and redemptive power, and especially not as a one-time past event but as Christ, present from primal beginnings to eschaton. Thus to talk about Christ as Word in our preaching is to consider how our little human words participate not just in the retelling of a history, but also in the evocation of the mythic past of creation and the mythic future of consummation.

Second, such a theology of the Word should impact how we understand preaching. If the Word is this event, this dynamic power summed up in the death and resurrection of Jesus Christ, then preaching should be not so much about giving past-tense book reports, but rather about *enacting the*

Word in the present. Here the scriptures once again point the way. Their forms can furnish us with frames for understanding how the Word would do what it does. Indeed, as first attempts at articulating the gospel, the scriptures' various dynamic forms can ground our preaching while calling us to speak the gospel into a new time and place. What is clear, however, is that preaching cannot merely be just another scientific report on the past. A word rendered only in the past tense of an objectified historical understanding runs the risk of being dead on arrival. By contrast, a view of the Word as enacted in preaching will embrace the ways the Bible preaches itself and can become a living testament to the gospel.[9]

Third, such a theology of the Word will also view hearers not as impediments to its action, but as codeterminants of it. If the old scientific method sought to keep the contemporary world out in order to avoid exegetical contamination, a theology of the Word that acknowledges what the Word does actually presupposes hearers who are addressed. If the text is not simply a past repository of fixed, static truth, then texts do not need to be protected from hearers. Indeed, if the Word is a dynamic force, it needs different hearers to continue to do its thing. Moreover, because hearers in all their diversity are the intended addressees of the Word, the Word itself changes according to time and place.

What is the upshot of this different theological understanding of the Word? For one thing, sermons don't always have to sound the same. If texts are not solely the result of some larger, determinative history, then we can first be attentive not solely to what they said (as historically determined), but to what they do (that is, how the text's Word would seek to *change* its historical context). Moreover, if preaching is not simply another book report on ancient uses of salt, or some dreary discourse about the biblical warrants for the eternal truth of the substitutionary theory of the atonement, then maybe the different things texts do can help us figure out what to do with our sermons. Finally, if our hearers are not the critical problem, but a hermeneutical invitation for the texts to address us again through our sermons, then we just may have a shared event on our hands.

Some examples may help. Imagine, for example, a sermon on the Beatitudes in Matthew 5:1–12 that did not turn this passage into a series of ethical injunctions: "We all *must* be meek, peacemakers, or pure in heart." Instead, the sermon might take its cue from what beatitudes do: namely, to *bless.* And what if a sermon on the parable of the prodigal son didn't make three didactic, objective points like some father-on-a-tirade, but ran parabolically down the road to embrace the scoundrel with the full-orbed hug of God's incalculable mercy? And what if a sermon on an apocalyptic text didn't sound like an attempt at a weather forecast, but overlaid images of the world we know with the world we are coming to know in Jesus Christ? Chances are, we would have a living, dynamic sermon.

APOCALYPTIC TEXTS: WHERE ARE THEY GOING?

The assumption of uniformity about what apocalypses say as an expression of historical context itself has a long history. Much scholarship in the field has been taken with the notion that some certain, prior historical situation or social grouping results in "apocalypticism" and apocalypses. In some cases, the focus is more on historical situations that engender the phenomenon: persecution, status/role discrepancy, or the threat of assimilation. Of course, the problem here is not that such analysis might be incorrect, but rather the assumption that apocalypses need always be a product of *one* of these. Similarly, many scholars have also argued that apocalypticism is a worldview of certain kinds of groups, which in turn produce apocalyptic writings. In some cases these groups may be characterized generally as sectarian or millenarian, or specifically as the hasidim, the zealots, the Essenes, or perhaps even the scribes. Again, the problem is not whether such historical and sociological investigations may show that such certain groups or historical situations may stand behind individual apocalypses, but the assumption that *all* apocalypses must be understood as produced by such a single group or in such a single historical moment. In other words, given the unusal phenomenon that is "apocalypticism," and derivatively, apocalypses, many scholars have been tempted to assert that its products are a unitary phenomenon subject to a simple unity of origins.

We need not assume, however, that the apocalyptic texts we deal with necessarily arise out of only one type of situation or group. Indeed, it is more critical to assume not the unity of apocalyptic origins, but precisely their diversity and variability. In fact, such a view of origins as being pure and singular is exactly the kind of myth that contemporary thinkers feel compelled to resist. French philosopher and iconoclast Michel Foucault puts it this way: "What is found at the historical beginning of things is not the inviolable identity of their origin; it is the dissension of other things. It is disparity."[10] So then, just because apocalyptic texts are unusual does not mean that only one type of unusual group could give them voice or that one unusual historical context could produce them. In his now classic text *The Apocalyptic Imagination,* John Collins demonstrated this quite ably for the whole corpus of Jewish apocalyptic literature.

The Jewish apocalypses were not produced by a single "apocalyptic movement. . . ." The problems to which these revelations are addressed vary in kind. An apocalypse can provide support in the face of persecution (such as, Daniel); reassurance in the face of culture shock (possibly the Book of the Watchers) or social powerlessness (the Similitudes of Enoch); reorientation in the wake of historical trauma (*2 Baruch, 3 Baruch*); consolation for the dismal fate of humanity (4 Ezra); or comfort for the inevitability of death (the *Testament of Abraham*).[11]

Preachers can open themselves to the many things apocalyptic texts do, both back then and now.

If Paul Ricoeur is right, much more is gained than lost with such a rich diversity in apocalyptic origins. Ricoeur calls it "the surplus of meaning."[12] For him, the interpretation of texts is important not because we recover a piece of someone else's past, but because it opens up new horizons of meaning in our present. Thus, Ricoeur claims, even when we give up a unified "original meaning," we actually gain so much more, for the sense of a text continues to make new meanings in ever-new contexts. As we approach a text to determine its "sense," it begins to move out to our world to disclose a "new way of being in the world," revealing an abundance of meaning that becomes evident from a new vantage point.[13]

From a preaching standpoint we have long known that a biblical text is not about just more historical information. Texts are not just things, but are actions, a *doing* that occasions a disclosure of the gospel. Apocalyptic texts come to us not because we are their first addressees (we're not), but because apocalyptic texts do something with the way we view the world. A recent two-framed public-service ad on the Toronto subway may help illustrate.[14] The first frame looks something like figure 1.

Figure 1

From the context (the ad genre in a public space where things are sold), we gather that the picture conforms to our normal (capitalistic) tunnel vision: something's for sale. Then comes the second frame and its caption (see figure 2).

Figure 2. **"Do you need a larger vision?"**

Biblical texts, especially apocalyptic ones, are valuable because they offer us an opportunity to enlarge *our* vision of the gospel beyond how we normally see things.

USING RHETORICAL CRITICISM
TO FIND OUT WHAT TEXTS DO

The practical question then becomes how we do it. How do we learn to read apocalyptic texts for what they do, and how they might "dis-close" our closed worlds? While we have a whole raft of methods to choose from, we will focus on one method by virtue of its simplicity and usefulness: rhetorical criticism.

Naturally, a turn to rhetoric here will raise concerns in some. In our age, the word "rhetoric" frequently appears after the word "just," as in, "What you are saying is just rhetoric." For the sake of understanding what apocalyptic texts do, however, we have to get past the rather dismissive take on language.[15]

As pastors we are already intuitively aware that parishioners rarely give us information just for the sake of passing on information. Say, for example, a parishioner says, "I just thought you should know that I have been the only adult minding the nursery for three weeks running." Any pastor knows that such a disclosure of pure information is not designed solely to inform, but to *do*. In a moment like that, a pastor is the focus of someone's persuasive discourse, as in, "Find some way to get me out of this nursery!"[16]

In fact, we instinctively use language all the time to persuade, or put colloquially, to do. If so, it may be useful to consider some of our more troublesome biblical texts from the same critical point of view and with the same pastoral sensitivity that we apply to the speech of our parishioners.

Contemporary biblical scholars give us some ideas for useful questions to ask texts as a way of discerning what they are up to rhetorically. The one I use below is a three-step method that I find particularly useful for preaching. It represents an abbreviated form of the method which classicist George Kennedy uses in his treatment of New Testament texts.[17] Yet perhaps the best way to learn how to apply rhetorical criticism to a text is simply to do it.

TOWARD OUR SERMONIC "DESTINATION": A RHETORICAL ANALYSIS OF MARK 13:24–37 (ADVENT 1B)

Step 1: Determine the Rhetorical Unit

From a preaching standpoint, this initial step is profoundly important. We may think that only an ivory tower exegete could ever care whether we have properly determined the boundaries of the text. But this is not so. For preachers who use rhetorical analysis, determining the boundaries is our first indication of our text's *destination*. It is our first opportunity to figure out where the text starts and where it is heading, that is, what it does.

From time to time lectionary committees determine pericope units for Sunday readings that do not correspond to the way a given discourse is rhetorically structured. Still, we probably should start with the lectionary text as is to see if the unit given is rhetorically useful.

[13:24] But in those days after that distress "the sun will be darkened, and the moon will not give its light, [25] and the stars will be falling from heaven, and the powers in the heavens will be shaken"; [26] then they will see Humanity's Child coming in the clouds with much power and glory. [27] Then he will send the angels and gather together his chosen ones from the four winds—from the edge of the earth to the edge of heaven. [28] From the fig tree learn the parable—when its branch becomes tender and shoots shoots, know that summer is near! [29] In the same way even you, when you all see these things happening, know that it is near—right at the door. [30] Truly I say to you all that this generation will not pass away until all these things happen. [31] Heaven and earth will pass away, but my words will not pass away. [32] But about the day or the hour, no one knows, neither the angels in heaven, nor the child, except the Parent. [33]

Watch out! Sleep with one eye open! For you do not know when the time is. [34] When a person going away from home leaves the house and gives the servants responsibility—to each one their job—they also command the doorman to keep watch. [35] Therefore, keep watch—for you do not know when the Lord of the house is coming—whether evening or midnight or at cock's crow or early morning, [36] lest he come suddenly and find you sleeping. [37] But what I say to you folks I say to all: Keep watch! (trans. mine)[18]

Our Text in the Context of Mark's Apocalyptic Discourse

Listening to our text, we can already discern one thing: we're entering Jesus' speech in the middle. The words tumble out without naming any context in which Jesus' discourse is taking place. Thus, if we have walked in on the middle of Jesus' apocalyptic speech, we should first ask where it began.

Any good exegesis of a lection like Jesus' apocalyptic speech in Mark should thus begin by seeing its connection to the immediate context in Mark. When we look closely, we see that our lection (Mark 13:24–37) is only part of a longer speech (Mark 13:5b–37). Mark's apocalyptic discourse, nearly a chapter long, will therefore make up the wider rhetorical horizon from which we consider our smaller unit, verses 24–37, in detail.

The question then arises: How do we know *this* is a rhetorical unit and not just some other arbitrary jumping-off point? The most obvious reason for considering Mark 13:5b–37 to be a larger rhetorical unit is that it represents a complete speech. Put plainly, Jesus starts speaking at the beginning (13:5b) and stops speaking after the end (14:1).

Another important reason for designating this apocalyptic discourse a rhetorical unit is the *change in time, place, and characters at either end of the speech*. In 13:3 Jesus moves from the Temple to the Mount of Olives across from it, implying a change of time and place. In addition, Jesus is asked a question in private (13:3), leaving only Peter, James, John, and Andrew as addressees for the speech. Afterward, the next move in the plot is signaled by a new time reference: "It was two days before the Passover" (Mark 14:1). The characters have also changed, shifting now to the high priests and scribes. Although not explicit, a change of place is also implied at 14:1ff.

Yet the most important reason for considering Mark 13:5b–37 to be a complete unit of speech is the presence of markers of beginning and ending within the speech itself.[19] Jesus' speech begins at 13:5b with a command verb: "watch" (Βλέπετε). The speech ends with another imperative

19

"watch" in verse 37 (γρηγορεῖτε). It was and often is still common to begin and end rhetorical units with a repetition of a key idea, word, or a cluster of key words. While a more obvious marker of beginning and end of the speech would repeat the same Greek word, Mark already begins revealing something of a "rhetorical intention," that is, what his language is trying to "do," through his *changing* of the verb of watching ("watch" = Βλέπετε in 13:5b and "watch" = γρηγορεῖτε in 13:37).

Mark 13:24–37 as a Rhetorical Subunit

Since we have determined that our lectionary text is only part of a larger rhetorical unit, the speech as a whole, we now turn to see *whether* our lection makes up an identifiable part of the discourse.

To be sure, the verb "watch" (Βλέπετε) and its synonyms (γρηγορεῖτε and ἴδε) are repeated often enough in this speech to allow for the determination of any number of rhetorical units or subunits ("watch" or Βλέπετὲ: vv. 5b, 9, 23, 33; "watch" or γρηγορεῖτε: vv. 34, 35, 37; "look" or ἴδε: vv. 1, 21). Yet our lectionary pericope marks off a distinct rhetorical subunit in a unique way. It begins by breaking open the "watch" (Βλέπετε) pattern of the first part of the speech by actually giving readers something to *see* (darkened sun, failing moon, and falling stars in vv. 24–25). This is followed by a shift from the command "Watch!" to the future-tense indicative "then they shall see . . . " in verse 26 (καὶ τότε ὄψονται). These changes, coupled with a heavy use of Βλέπετε and its synonyms at the end of the unit (vv. 33, 34, 35, and 37), indicate that our text represents a subunit of the longer speech.

Setting our lectionary text within the rhetorical intention that we discerned for the whole speech, we discover how our subunit tries to flesh out the new way of "watching" we discussed earlier. In verse 24 we are given something to "see" (sun, moon, stars, Humanity's Child, and the gathering angels) that leads to a new kind of watching by the end of the speech. Our discernment of how the rhetorical unit is set up already points us toward a possible homiletical destination: the rhetoric of the text wants hearers to "watch" in a new way.

Step 2: Analyze the Rhetorical Arrangement of the Text

Rhetorical arrangement is concerned with the order of the speech's arguments. We are simply disussing the arrangement of a speech's persuasive case. If I, for example, wish to persuade someone that barbecue from Tennessee is better than barbecue from Texas, I would first need to find the best reasons to lay out for my case (for example, the superiority of certain

Tennessee vinegar-based sauces to Texas tomato-based ones and the relative tastiness of pulled pork shoulder in comparison to beef). Nonetheless, having good arguments to make a case is never enough. A good rhetorician must put them in an order that is optimally persuasive to her hearers. A speaker may wish to begin with the strongest argument or end with a bang by saving the strongest reason for last. A speaker may also want to disarm the hearers (let's assume for the moment they are Texans) with a narrative that reduces their defensiveness about the local barbecue (perhaps a funny, homespun story about Sam Houston would do). From the example we can begin to see why arrangement is important. Rhetorical analysis that focuses on the arrangement or order of Jesus' apocalyptic speech will help reveal what the discourse is trying to do.

We begin by recalling that our lection begins and ends with an altered view of "watching." The order should help us make sense of how the speech does its work of helping us "watch" in a different way. Let us consider the speech's topics and how it organizes them. This means again paying special attention to the role of verses 24–37 in the wider apocalyptic discourse of Mark 13.

> Beginning: **Watch** (Βλέπετε) that you are not misled (v. 5b–6).
> Topic A: **Watch** out (Βλέπετε) for false signs (vv. 5b–8).
> > 1. When (ὅταν) you hear of wars . . . *don't fear* (vv. 7–8).
> Topic B: **Watch** out (βλέπετε) for yourselves (vv. 9–22).
> > 1. When (ὅταν) they hand you over, *don't worry* (vv. 11ff.).
> > 2. When (ὅταν) you see the abomination, *flee* (vv. 14ff.).
> > 3. When (τότε ἐάν) one says: look (ἴδε), *don't believe* (vv. 21f.).
> Middle: But you **watch** (βλέπετε); for I have told you everything (v. 23).
> Topic C: **. . . then they will see** (ὄψονται) Humanity's Child (vv. 24–27).
> Analogy: Learn the lesson of the fig tree (vv. 28–32).
> > 1. When (ὅταν) the fig tree . . . , *know* (v. 28b).
> > 2. When (ὅταν) you see these things . . . , *know* (v. 29).
> > 3. Truly . . . this generation will not pass . . . , but *no one knows* the hour . . . except the Parent (vv. 30ff.).
> Topic D:
> > A **Watch** (βλέπετε), **sleep with one eye open** (ἀγρυπνεῖτε) (v. 33a)

B For *you do not know* when (πότε) the time is (v. 33b)

C As one charges a doorman to **watch** (γρηγορῇ) (v. 34)

C′ **Therefore watch** (γρηγορεῖτε) (v. 35a)

B′ For *you do not know* when (πότε) the Lord is coming (vv. 35bf.)

A′ **Watch** (γρηγορεῖτε) (v. 37).

End: But what I say to you folks I say to all: keep **watch** (γρηγορεῖτε) (v. 37)!

The arrangement confirms the rhetorical intention that began to emerge when we determined the boundaries of the unit in step 1. Note the importance of the key word "watch" for the structure of the entire apocalyptic discourse. For the first half of the speech, the command form "Watch!" serves as a repetition device to draw attention to the kind of watching required to ensure not being misled, namely, watching for false signs (vv. 5bff.) and watching for yourselves (vv. 9ff.) Moreover, every "watch" imperative is followed by "when" statements that lead to negative advice: for example, *"don't* fear." The section that associates "watch" (βλέπετε) is then closed off with the final combination of watch/mislead in verse 23.

Viewed within this arrangement, our lectionary text (vv. 24–37) then begins with a different verb of seeing (ὄψονται), although the verb comes near the end of a long, complex sentence (v. 26). The "seeing" verb—its tense, its voice, and its person—has changed. We have been "watching," but now toward the end of a long sentence, *they* shall "see"—and what they see is an apocalyptic scene that symbolically envisions some kind of eschatological salvation.

What comes next? The "when" sentences use the analogy of the fig tree (v. 28b) and "these things" (v. 29) as the basis for issuing a new command: "know that summer is near!" This new seeing marks a shift to *positive* advice. Finally, the old word "watch" (βλέπετε) is taken up again in Topic D, but joined up with new words—words of *active* watching (at v. 33 βλέπετε is joined immediately with αγρυπνεῖτε and subsequently to γρηγορεῖτε) while also being connected with an analogy of household servants continuing to do their work. The watching is called for in connection with the statement that one does not know "when." The text changes from the indefinite when (ὅταν, as in "whenever") to the more definite when (πότε, a point in time for all this to happen). Through the arrangement of the speech both what we are watching for and the quality of our "watching" have been altered. The key is verse 24. We expect another "watch" in the series that began with 13:5b, but instead we are given something to "see," an apocalyptic scene of gathering the elect (13:27).

The final "watch" in the conclusion gives us a new understanding of what the speech means. We do not need to "watch out" here in the sense of the negative advice of the first half of the speech (13:5b–23); we are to keep watch for salvation.

For us who preach, this rhetorical analysis is beginning to bring us toward a sermon. Where do our congregations experience a "watch out" dread? Many already live their ecclesial lives as if their best years were behind them. Sometimes the disappointment that the Sunday school is not as full as it was thirty years ago and that the sanctuary has more gray hair than not leaves a church in a perennial "watch out" mode. We live in a culture of profound suspicion. Yet God will not be contained, even by our experiences of cultural disappointment. Where in the texture of our common life might we watch for a surprising incursion of Jesus' salvific presence? Perhaps the task of the preacher is to identify places where Christ is already coming among us and the world outside our walls.

Step 3: Analyze the Text's Arguments and Style

In this third step we consider more closely what kinds of arguments are used in the speech and how they are worded. Again, this is no unimportant matter.

If, continuing with the previous barbecue example, I choose for an argument the inherent superiority of the state of Tennessee to the Republic of Texas, I am not likely to win many adherents in Dallas. The kinds of arguments I choose are important.

By the same token, the style I use, that is, how I say what I say, will either enhance or detract from what I say. If, say, I want to share with a congregation the overwhelming way in which God lavishes on us grace upon grace, it would not help me to do so in short, staccato sentences. For that matter, if my face is contorted in anger with veins visibly protruding, I can talk about God's unmerited mercy until I'm blue in the face, but my hearers will find it hard to believe if my style and the content of my speech are at cross purposes.

Turning to our lection, we begin by noting that the arguments used in Mark 13:24–37 appeal to different types of evidence. The speech uses scripture quotes as "external" warrants (external because the quotes exist apart from the speech) and develops new arguments as warrants internal to the speech (internal because the speaker has developed his own analogies, illustrations, and examples from nature).

Our lection begins with external evidence. Verses 24–27 use many scriptural allusions (Isa. 13:10; Ezek. 32:7–8; Joel 2:10, 31; 3:15; Dan. 7:13–14). Because of their connection to scripture, they would have likely added to the authoritativeness of the speech for the hearers/readers of Mark's Gospel.

The subsequent arguments in verses 28–37, however, are largely made up of internal evidence. The parable of the fig tree and the story of the householder on a journey are compelling because they draw on things we know in nature and in life.

By moving from external evidence (scripture allusions) to internal evidence (parables and stories) in the way it does, the speech makes the notion of Jesus' return visually immanent or present to hearers (vv. 24–27), while denying that we know it to be temporally imminent in an absolute sense (13:28ff.). The fig tree parable and the story of the returning householder do the work of showing this return as something near. *Yet they both end emphatically with the idea that the point in time of the parousia is unknown.* Their familiarity as analogies from the world we know, one of changing seasons and returning householders, is perhaps deceiving. The unit starts off with vivid description as a rather bald statement of what "they shall see" and then proceeds to buttress the claim by arguing ostensibly from nature and everyday life. The structured argumentation of the speech seems to disorient and reorient hearers to a different kind of apocalyptic reality. In other words, it shakes us up regarding what we think we know.

The style of the apocalyptic speech is marked by some peculiarities. After the careful organization of topics A and B and their closure with the second person command to "watch" (βλέπετε) in verse 23, the switch to third person verbs disorients the hearers ("then they shall see . . ." = ὄψονται). Such a move may be an example of a deliberate misuse of language.

Another part of the speech turns from the descriptive vision to direct address. Verses 24–27 are in the third person (they, he, etc.), yet verses 28–37 switch to the second person ("you" in the plural imperative). Such a shift in addressees would have been noticed by hearers. Stylistically, the speech then reorients its hearers by turning to them in direct speech.

At various points the speech also uses complex, multiclausal sentences. Verses 24–27 introduce the parousia only after a long description of the apocalyptic convulsions of the cosmos. For hearers this would feel like a rhetoric of delay. The same thing happens in verse 32, where a list of those who do not know the hour ends with the one who does know: the "Parent." A similar rhetoric of delay also marks verse 34 (where the main verb and subordinate clause appear at the end) and verses 35–36, an exceedingly complex, multiclausal sentence in Greek.

In both the kinds of arguments used and the way they are said, Mark's Gospel seems to be trying to reorient hearers in verses 24–37. The change in repetition and the rhetoric of delay in verses 24–27 cause us to reconsider what we are "watching" for. The use of complex sentences and the switch to internal evidence and direct second person speech seem to move us toward reorienting the quality of our "watching." As a result, the rhetorical invention and style work hand in hand with the rhetorical arrangement to produce an unmistakably unified effect. Mark's Gospel wishes us to watch differently, not just in terms of what or whom we await, but in how we do so, that is, how we understand watching in relation to time.

RHETORIC OF TEXT
AND RHETORIC OF SERMON

So how does the lection's rhetoric play out homiletically? Three aspects come immediately to mind.

First, the rhetoric seems to want to move us from one kind of watching to another. The speech starts with the standard "watch out" rhetoric that we would expect from an apocalyptic speech (Mark 13:5). Doubtless our hearers would notice that. Yet the kind of "watching" that the text's rhetoric leads us to is different: a praxis-oriented watching that "sleeps with one eye open" for the new thing God is doing. This kind of watching is not passively fearful but active and expectant. Already this rhetorical *doing* can begin stirring our imaginations. To what extent is our eschatological watching a kind of passive "Look out!"? And where is our watching a kind of leaning into the future which God both "knows" and gives? As we answer these questions, the doing of the text may already be starting to show how our sermon might do something similar.

Second, the "seeing" that the rhetoric calls forth focuses on an apocalyptic scene of salvation (vv. 24–27). Here the negative advice of "watch out, don't . . . " gives way to positive advice: "Know this!" Thus, if the rhetoric first invites us to shift from passive to active watching, its object also shifts from negative dangers to something that is positively visionary. But with this analysis of the rhetoric a theological question arises for preachers. Just what are you waiting for: a cosmic cataclysm or the advent of God's salvation? Consequently, the rhetoric of the speech also invites hearers into a kind of theological discernment about the object of their "watching," too.

Third, the rhetoric shifts our idea of the nature of watching from something temporally "imminent" (temporally near as a point in time) to something mythically and visually "immanent" (spatially near in the sense of "whenever" something happens, like summer). Theologically, this shift in the language of time moves away from the literalness of apocalyptic timetables and moves toward a more proleptic sense: the "end" is already beginning to emerge, even if not yet here in all its fullness. Whenever such things happen (just as a few fig leaves point to summer), we know Christ is near. New Testament scholar Ched Myers offers this explanation of the distinction Mark's rhetoric draws here:

> Mythical time, however, is not conceived of chronologically (chronos) but archetypically (kairos). The two "ages" coexist in human history as "good" and "evil," each with their own respective "pasts" and "futures." The function of the myth is parenetic: the dualism compels listeners to clarify their allegiances in the historical struggle between fundamentally differing social visions. . . . The collapsing of chronos into kairos is not, however, absolute in Biblical faith: Yahweh's purposes will "in the end" prevail. Apocalyptic dualism is not static but dynamic, asserting that the corrupt age is already "passing away," the new one dawning.[20]

Again, this shift in the rhetoric invites us to begin reflecting homiletically about our own world. Where does the "whenever" (ὅταν) of God's ultimate salvific purposes emerge even now—even if only in fragments, that is, proleptically? Where do we see in bits and pieces something of God's new creation?

Therefore, our homiletical destination with Mark 13:24–37 is a new kind of watching. The difference is that this rhetorically effected watching is not passive, but active; not focused on what we ought to avoid, but on what God is doing; and not oriented to a distant future, but to a proleptic present where God's intentions are already emerging in small signs of salvific presence.

In traditions of sacramental presence, one might talk about profound symbols of God coming to us in our common life. The key is to avoid saying how we're *supposed* to feel about Eucharist. Yet how can we describe concretely the eucharistic moment so it doesn't sound like (1) the official statement from denominational headquarters or (2) an intrasubjective account about how we're obligated to feel about the body and blood? Inviting congregations to a new way of "seeing" Christ coming may mean thinking about the eucharistic symbols socially. From there, the preacher may want to extrapolate Christ's surprising presence to the world about us.

There is a chance that Jesus continues to come and eat with sinners and we don't even see it . . . yet.

Sound interesting? Can you begin to imagine how the rhetoric of the text might help you do something similar in your sermon? Yet before we head off for our homiletical "destination," it might help to consider how we can help our hearers get there. It is time to see how the form of our apocalyptic texts can shape the homiletical route to a new kind of "watching."

---

1. Krister Stendahl formulated this classic division of labor between a historical-critical approach to the New Testament and practical theology ("Biblical Theology, Contemporary," in *The Interpreter's Dictionary of the Bible* vol. 1, ed. George Arthur Buttrick [Nashville: Abingdon, 1962] 418–31).

2. The notion of meaning as "event" is hardly new. Building on the work of the later Heidegger, for whom language was the "House of Being," the representatives of the new hermeneutic offered a framework for understanding Word of God as a "word event" whereby we understand *through* language (Paul Achtemeier, *An Introduction to the New Hermeneutic* [Philadelphia: Westminster, 1969], 86–100). Although the new hermeneutic collapsed, in part because of its ties to a now dated existentialism, Paul Ricoeur subsequently resurrected a dialectic between event and meaning (*Interpretation Theory: Discourse and the Surplus of Meaning* [Fort Worth: Texas Christian Univ. Press, 1976], 8–12).

3. Discerning readers will note that yelling "Fire!" does presuppose a prior context of combustion. This cannot be denied. What we are suggesting here is not a jettisoning of historical concerns (was there *really* a fire, or not?) but a shifting of primary orientation. Christian proclamation is at bare minimum an event in language between preachers and hearers. In focusing our exegetical concerns on the space between a text and its readers/hearers, we may just be getting an angle of vision more suited to the nature of the preaching task itself. We are not "writing objective history" when we preach and hear, we are rather engaged in a theological activity akin to "faith seeking understanding." In this way, a Bible text that yells "Fire!" may just be an invitation for us to discern what may be so combustible about our world, too—and what we are called to be or do in relation to that world.

4. Norman Peterson argues that such an understanding of historical criticism is actually a form of "historicism" (*Literary Criticism for New Testament Critics* [Philadelphia: Fortress, 1978], 25–33).

5. David Randolph, *The Renewal of Preaching* (Philadelphia: Fortress, 1969).

6. To be sure, Craddock was concerned that mere imitation of biblical forms would be trite (*As One without Authority* [Nashville: Abingdon, 1971], 153). Nonetheless, he offers it as a suggestive option for preachers trying to break the hold that deductively shaped sermons have traditionally had on the preacher's mind.

7. Eugene Lowry argues that narrative sermons can be used whether or not one follows the plot of a given biblical narrative (*The Homiletical Plot* [Atlanta: John Knox, 1980]). Henry Mitchell considers the narrative sermon as a specific genre available to the preacher (*Celebration and Experience in Preaching* [Nashville: Abingdon, 1990], 87–100). Wayne Robinson complements the work of these two figures with edited essays and sermons on narrative preaching from a variety of

perspectives including his own (*Journeys toward Narrative Preaching* [New York: Pilgrim, 1990).

8. David Buttrick argues that sermons can vary according to biblical texts because the "intending" of the texts "in consciousness" likewise varies (*Homiletic: Moves and Structures* [Philadelphia: Fortress, 1987], 285–363). Thomas G. Long considers how part of the rhetoric of diverse biblical forms in their own communicative contexts can be used for the shaping of sermons in the contemporary context (*Preaching and the Literary Forms of the Bible* [Philadelphia: Fortress, 1989]).

9. The Reformation theologian Martin Luther deals with this issue in two ways. First, a mere statement of past fact does no one any good. Theologically, it may not matter whether God has created the world as pure fact. Any such statement must ultimately for Luther be understood as "*pro me,*" for me (or, as I prefer, for us). Second, Luther understands the New Testament not so much as "scripture" but as "preaching." In the end, the Word happens not because we read an ancient text but because we hear the Word in preaching. Faith, for Luther, is an acoustical affair, the work of Word and Spirit in the here and now. Indeed, preaching is where there is a "setting forth of Christ . . . never a mere narration of historical happenings" (Phillip S. Watson, *Let God Be God: An Interpretation of the Theology of Martin Luther* [London: Epworth, 1947], 151).

10. Michel Foucault, *Language, Counter-Memory, Practice,* ed. Donald F. Bouchard, trans. Donald F. Bouchard and Sherry Simon (Ithaca, N.Y.: Cornell Univ. Press, 1977), 114.

11. John Collins, *The Apocalyptic Imagination,* 2d ed. (Grand Rapids: Eerdmans, 1998), 280.

12. Ricoeur posits his "surplus of meaning" where a text is distanced from its producer through the act of writing, and thus its sense from its original reference. For Ricoeur this "distanciation" is not problematic but productive (*Interpretation Theory,* 44).

13. Ibid., 37, 89–95.

14. I owe this illustration to Rev. Michael Rattee, a homiletics graduate student at the University of Toronto.

15. How odd that we use rhetoric in order to dismiss its usefulness! New Testament scholars take pains to say that the study of rhetoric considers the effectiveness of various means of persuasion (George A. Kennedy, *New Testament Interpretation through Rhetorical Criticism* [Chapel Hill: Univ. of North Carolina Press, 1984], 3; Burton L. Mack, *Rhetoric and the New Testament* [Minneapolis: Fortress, 1990], 15). By denouncing a discourse as "just rhetoric," we actually are making a quintessentially rhetorical statement—and one designed persuasively to "do."

16. One could, of course, imagine contexts in which such words might mean something else, say, "Look at me, I've broken the record for consecutive weeks in the nursery!" Or perhaps, "Your preaching is lousy: thank God for the relative solace of the nursery on Sunday morning!" Regardless of the contextual variations, however, such speech is rarely given in just a neutral, informational sense. Chances are, such disclosures are designed to do, or better, designed to convince you to do something (for example, offer congratulations for the former, or retool your homiletical skills for the latter).

17. Kennedy uses a four-step method that also considers the rhetorical situation of the text (*Rhetorical Criticism,* 33–38). While such information is undoubtedly

28

helpful in discerning what rhetoric is doing in a given discourse, I am not so san-
guine about the transparency of a discourse to its "situation."

18. However awkwardly, I have tried to render the text in as inclusive a fashion as
I could. As a recovering sexist and a sympathizer in the cause of the liberation
of women, I freely acknowledge that my translation choices are far from perfect.
Readers may notice how I also try to lift out forms in the second person plural.
I use the rather Southern sounding "you all" or "you folks" to indicate the second person plural in the Greek. The most technically problematic aspect of my
translation is the use of the term "Humanity's Child" for the traditional "Son of
Man." By translating the term this way, I am not only trying to make this christological appellation more inclusive, but also understanding the term as meaning a representative figure for the new humanity. Child, for me, evokes the
newness of the new age. Of course, the debate as to the meaning of the term "Son
of Man" is as long running as it is contentious. Those wishing to review both the
various positions and the inherently dual aspect of the Markan "Son of Man"
designation may wish to start with Hugh Anderson's *The Gospel of Mark,* New
Century Bible Commentary (Grand Rapids: Eerdmans, 1976), 208–13. For a
more up-to-date treatment of the topic, readers may wish to consult a fine article by George W. E. Nickelsburg, "Son of Man," in *The Anchor Bible Dictionary* vol. 6, ed. David Noel Friedman (New York: Doubleday, 1992), 137–50.

19. George Kennedy calls such markers of opening and closure to a speech *inclu-
sios (Rhetorical Criticism,* 34)

20. Ched Myers, *Binding the Strong Man* (Maryknoll, N.Y.: Orbis, 1988), 338–39.

Chapter 3

How in the World We Get There: Genre, Forms, and Apocalyptic Texts

Imagine that someone comes up to you and out of the blue says two simple words: "Knock, knock." How would you respond? What would you answer to the phrase "Knock, knock"?

Nine times out of ten you would come back with "Who's there?" Even some precocious children as young as two know the joke: "Knock, knock" just naturally summons forth our "Who's there?"

How is it that we know the rules of a knock-knock joke? We may have overheard such jokes when we were young. Perhaps we first read them in a joke book. Whatever it was, we caught on to the form of the knock-knock joke by means of the social conventions of language.

So what does a knock-knock joke have to do with our dreaded apocalyptic texts? They are both "forms." Both are instances of patterned communication. Having said that, we must also admit an obvious difference between a knock-knock joke and an apocalyptic text: while we know the knock-knock joke form by heart, we do not know much about apocalyptic forms. Chances are we learned our "Knock, knock" long before the apocalyptic "Behold, I stand at the door and knock" (Rev. 3:20, RSV). We are much more likely to get the form of the knock-knock joke than we are the form of an apocalyptic text.

Of course, talking about "form" almost always raises homiletical hackles. No doubt many of us are averse to focusing on matters of form. Form sounds like "formal." Form is the opposite of the weighty "content." Form is for bureaucrats, experts on manners, academics, and other such people—not parish pastors trying to get up a Sunday sermon.

Actually, we use forms of patterned communication in our daily lives all the time. When a parishioner comes out of the sanctuary Sunday after Sunday, year after year, and shakes your hand saying rather flatly, "Nice sermon, pastor," you eventually come to expect it. If, suddenly, one Sunday the parishioner says nothing at the end of the service, you instinctively know from the deviation in "form" in this interpersonal communication in the narthex that it's time to pay a call to find out what's up. If, by way of contrast, the same parishioner were to come out of church some Sunday, shake your hand, and say with uncharacteristic abandon, "I heard the gospel today, pastor," you will probably surmise that something powerful has registered through your sermon. Either way, the *variation* of the customary communication form "Nice sermon, pastor" speaks volumes.

New Testament scholar James Bailey discusses patterns of communication and their variations in forms. With a clever appeal to personal relations, he helps bring the power of such simple communicative forms to life:

> For example, a young woman repeatedly writes letters to her boyfriend, beginning each letter "Dearest Eric" and closing with "All my love, Anne." Then one day Eric receives a letter from Anne that begins "Dear Eric" and simply ends "Yours truly, Anne." *The modified form creates a dramatically different impact on Eric.* (emphasis mine)[1]

Forms can be helpful to understand, because forms generate a set of expectations that have an impact on hearers.

Of course, there's more to any form than just learning it in language. Indeed, we learned early on that the form of the knock-knock joke is the vehicle for what the joke does. If jokes rhetorically effect laughter, the form of the joke, in this case the knock-knock variety, is the how by which that laughter is done.

Therefore, in this chapter our focus shifts from *what* apocalyptic texts do to *how* they do it. In doing so we will also begin to explore the implications of the forms of apocalyptic texts for preaching.

FORM AND BIBLICAL TEXT

Why should forms matter to us homiletically? Two good reasons come immediately to mind. First, our biblical preaching texts (usually pericopes and other lectionary snippets) are not just repositories of cognitive information, but works whose forms are part of the communicative package.[2]

Second, our sermons are not generic carriers of salvific factoids, but are themselves borne by their homiletical shape. Naturally, each of these assertions deserves some attention before we look at apocalyptic forms and the genre apocalypse up close.

In order to talk about the relation of form and text, we need to begin with a caveat. We are not looking at matters of form to get at an original community or the oral history behind a text, as many classically trained biblical form critics are wont to do. As preachers/exegetes we are looking at form *relative to its homiletical value,* not as an open window to some community that produced it.

Form criticism as an exegetical method assumed that the text represented an oral form that was used in a specific community. When looking at these forms, critics hoped to be able to determine their typical setting in the life of the community (German: *Sitz im Leben*). From there they would be in a position to understand something more about the community that produced it, how the form functioned in that community, and perhaps even something of its preliterary oral history.[3]

By relating matters of form to a biblical text we will be conducting a close reading of biblical forms for the sake of their homiletical impact on hearers. While information about the communities behind them will be helpful, they will not be our end destination. Thus, for example, when we encounter a biblical scene where patriarchs and matriarchs meet at a well and end up courting (such as Isaac and Rebekah, Jacob and Rachel, Moses and the seven daughters of the Midianite priest, etc.), we won't just dredge up dusty old histories of nomadic watering practices and bucolic struggles over water rights and assume we've interpreted the form. Nor will we summon the ghosts of tales told around a desert campfire and assume we've thereby explained our love story at the well. Instead, we will look at the form of the story, and explain it in terms of what it uses (an extra character — say, another sister — plot elements, scene) and what it loses (who initiates the conversation, who marries whom, etc.). By comparing how our text "con-forms" to its typical shape and how it does not, we can focus on the form's unique impact on hearers. A helpful way to consider matters of the form of a text with respect to its communicative impact would be to see which elements of the typical form are present and which are absent. Or, from a hearing community's point of view, where are the form's expectations *met* and where are they *thwarted*?

Of course, it might help to see such odd notions of form in action.

Knock, knock.
Who's there?

Ida.
Ida who?
Not Ida who, Idaho.

Conventional? Painfully so. But now try this one:

Knock, knock.
Who's there?
A rabbi, a priest, and a Presbyterian minister.

Notice how the first joke stays within the conventional form of the knock-knock joke. We know the rules of the joke, and the punch line (though tedious) proceeds within the horizon of expectation of the joke — it *meets* our normal expectations of the knock-knock joke. The second joke, by contrast, breaks with the form on purpose. In answering the question "Who's there?" with a standard introductory phrase of another joke genre, we have subverted the form by drawing attention to the joke form itself. Though we began with the knock-knock joke, our expectations of the joke's typical form were *thwarted*. Clearly the impact of the execution of the two forms on hearers is different.

Our angle of vision on biblical forms focuses on how they accomplish their purposes in relation to hearers' expectations. In short, in this study we look at biblical forms not for the history *behind* the form but for the auditory impact in front of it.

FORM AND SERMON

Sermons themselves represent genres and use forms within their internal development (illustrations, examples, images). In our day, sermonic genres can vary widely. Nonetheless, there are certain generic features of sermons that hearers use as interpretive guides for hearing.

For example, hearers listening to a three-point sermon that begins with the phrase "My first point is that we should love our families" will likely not expect the sermon to end there. Hearers, having heard the words "my first point," will expect to hear, a few more minutes into the sermon: "as for my second point. . . . " By introducing numbered points as a structuring device, preachers generate a horizon of expectation for the hearers. From there on out, the sermon negotiates meaning by either meeting those formal expectations (offering point 2) or thwarting them (dropping the enumeration).

The importance of hearers' horizon of expectation also applies to un-enumerated homiletic genres like narrative sermons. If, for example, a narrative preacher's sermons follow a standard fourfold plot (conflict, complication, reversal, and outcome, or denouement), hearers will eventually learn the genre and come to expect it. In this way narrative sermons, like others, also *generate* a horizon of expectation that can either be met by following the plot or thwarted by omitting part of the plot (say, the outcome) in the course of the sermon.

On the broadest level, the hearers' horizon of expectation also comes into play for every sermon at the introduction. As some have noted, sermon introductions often function as a promise, even a "contract," for hearing.[4] However much or little a preacher discloses at the sermon's introduction, the frame that it sets enables the hearers to determine what to expect, or not expect, in a sermon.

It is also true that the very *choice* of sermon form has a communicative impact on hearers. A sermon that proceeds by rationally numbered points most likely will say that the world is an ordered place where we know the gospel and what it means. This may be why the deductive sermon remains popular in some circles even to this day. By contrast, narrative sermons might stay with the fourfold narrative form of conflict, complication, reversal, and outcome but vary from week to week as to how the reversal happens (for example, one week a reversal of circumstances, the next, a change in perspective of the protagonist). In such a case the gospel comes through what is "known" in the horizon of expectation, but it surprises the hearer nonetheless. In yet another option, a sermon genre or formal element in it might be abandoned and thus subvert the horizon of expectation altogether. In this case, the gospel is understood as completely discontinuous from our expectations and conventions.[5] Theologian Karl Barth comes close to this understanding of the gospel in his arguments against the practice of sermon introductions.[6]

FORMAL TRAINING IN APOCALYPSES

Since both texts and sermons meld form with content, we need to go back to square one. We require an understanding of the genre apocalypse and the smaller forms related to it. Apocalypses are made up of forms that we rarely, if ever, learn in our culture. Therefore, we need to study enough of them so we can track what expectations they intend to awake in hearers. If we immerse ourselves in the form of apocalyptic texts, they are less likely to elude us and more likely to help us preach.

First we must determine what belongs and what does not. That is, we must address the question of the forms and their relationship to the genre apocalypse.

One distinction is especially worth noting. When we talk about forms that make up the genre apocalypse, we should not use the words "form" and "genre" interchangeably. For the sake of clarity, here the word "genre" when used in referring to an apocalypse refers to the level of a whole work. Thus, the New Testament is composed of several genres: Gospels (Matthew, Mark, Luke, and John), some letters (Romans, Galatians, etc.), and one apocalypse (Revelation).[7] By contrast, we are using the term "form" to describe the literary parts that make up the larger works. Thus, for example, the genre of the Gospels contains forms like parables, pronouncement stories, healing stories, crucifixion scenes, and commissioning narratives. The genre of the letter contains its own forms (greeting, thanksgiving, body, paranesis, closing) and even incorporates other, smaller forms into its body (for example, household codes, lists of virtues and vices, allegories, confessions, quotations from the Hebrew Bible). The genre of apocalypse, like Revelation, can also have many different forms within it: letters to the seven churches, throne-room visions, judgment scenes, theophanies. Therefore, we will use the term "genre" to describe a whole work and the term "form" to refer to the subunits within the work.

Another example of this distinction can be seen in the way different genres of movies use forms to do their work. Few would likely dispute that the Western movie genre is quite different from the detective/mystery movie genre. Typically, the Western is set in the old West, features characters like sheriffs, outlaws, and ranchers, and has a plot that moves toward some violent confrontation between good (the white-hatted characters) and evil (the black-hatted ones). By contrast, the detective/mystery movie has its own distinctive generic components: usually the setting is a twentieth-century one, the protagonists are sleuths, victims, and potential suspects, and the plot moves toward an unveiling of the criminal in a powerful recognition scene.

We notice in our list above that the distinctiveness of the two movie genres is conveyed by elements like setting, character, and formal elements of the plot (shoot-out scene vs. recognition scene). On one level we can instinctively intuit how movie genres differ. Yet it is also true that genres share certain features as well—even formal ones like "type scenes."[8] In fact, one typical form that both the Western and detective/mystery genres can share is the chase scene. In the chase scene, the sheriff/hero or the detective/sleuth either pursues or is pursued by some antagonist(s). The primary difference is that in the Western it usually happens on horseback (think of how many times the Lone Ranger gallops across the screen in those old films) and in most detective/mystery movies the chase scene uses motorized vehicles.

From this we can see how genre and form interrelate. Genres, which describe a typical shape at the level of the whole work, use forms within them to further their plot lines or lines of argument. In some cases the forms used in genres are unique; in others the forms are shared across genres. Either way, we experience a form as being helpful for establishing a horizon of expectation for what might happen in a given movie scene (for example, the phrase "the butler did it" in the recognition scene of a detective/mystery film) or at the level of a whole work (the white-hatted good guys will somehow overcome the black-hatted minions of evil in the Western genre).

Yet even when we grasp the distinction between form and genre described above, it may not immediately be apparent how this relates to apocalyptic texts that appear in our lectionaries. We must keep the distinction between form and genre clear because apocalyptic texts do not show up solely in John's Apocalypse. Indeed, as preachers of the gospel, we find ourselves contending with apocalyptic texts throughout the three-year lectionary cycle. Sometimes the text comes from the New Testament representative of the apocalyptic genre, Revelation. On other occasions a New Testament lection is an apocalyptic form embedded in another genre (for example, the apocalyptic discourse of Mark 13, which is a form used in the Gospel). Then again, the imported apocalyptic material could be as wispy as an unrelated text featuring an individual motif (such as teachings about "resurrection" or parables about the "kingdom of God"). We know, therefore, that some apocalyptic forms show up in both the Gospel genre (Mark 13:24–27; Matt. 24:29–31; Luke 21:25–27) and in the letter genre (1 Thess. 4:16–17). Thus, if we wish to preach faithfully with apocalyptic texts, we must look beyond Revelation, even if its genre is helpful for understanding the forms that make it up.[9]

Fortunately, we do not need to start from scratch. Recent studies have sought to determine the genre apocalypse and its attendant forms. After a careful reading of extant texts, the Apocalypse Group of the Society of Biblical Literature Genres Project came up with a nuanced definition of the genre, which we discussed in the Introduction. The beauty of that definition is that it sets clear parameters for the genre, even while accounting for the diversity of apocalypses. Yet the definition also accomplishes something even more useful for the kind of formal study we will undertake here: it provides a baseline for understanding our New Testament apocalypse (Revelation) and those texts which do not manifest the whole genre, but represent what the Apocalypse Group called "related works" (Mark 13 or Qumran scrolls). The result is that we can place texts from Revelation and apocalyptic texts from other biblical books, such as 1 Thessalonians

4:13–18, within a context that can help us understand the "horizon of expectation" that the given form is designed to evoke. In short, by comparing certain apocalyptic texts in the Bible with similar texts in historically prior and contemporaneous apocalypses, we can figure out how to respond to the "Knock, knock" of a given apocalpytic text.[10]

Criteria for Using Apocalyptic Texts as a Literary Baseline

In order to use these apocalypses fruitfully as a baseline for getting the "Knock, knock" of apocalyptic forms and genres in the New Testament, we will also need to learn to use them with some critical care. Two restrictions will help us to focus our investigations: (1) limiting our focus to Jewish apocalypses and (2) narrowing that focus to Jewish apocalypses either contemporaneous with or prior to our biblical texts. As a rule this will limit us to writings that can be dated no later than the end of the first century.[11]

As for the first restriction, why should we focus exclusively on *Jewish* apocalypses? At first glance such an exclusively Jewish orientation appears arbitrary. Are there not non-Jewish literary parallels that would help make sense of New Testament apocalyptic texts? Besides, would not Gentile converts to the early Christian movement have heard apocalyptic texts with Gentile, as opposed to Jewish, ears?

The problem is that such questions unnecessarily dichotomize things into either Jewish or Greco-Roman. In all likelihood, the people we call early Christians would have been viewed as falling within the orbit of Judaism and not as a separate Gentile "church" until late in the first century. Moreover, many of those involved in the early Christian movement would have been attracted to it precisely because of the broad religious appeal of Judaism to many Gentiles. Early converts would likely have become familiar with Jewish apocalyptic figures and writings which had both broad appeal and varying provenance.[12] Most important, however, is the value of seeing New Testament apocalyptic texts specifically within a Jewish literary matrix precisely because of the dominant Hellenistic context. John Collins has argued that the many different apocalyptic writings (Egyptian, Persian) in the Greco-Roman context represent culture-specific reactions in and against Hellenism.[13] In other words, different cultures drew on their own fund of myths and symbols when they developed apocalyptic writings to counter the domination of Hellenism. If this is the case, then the primary literary milieu for reading New Testament apocalyptic materials should be Jewish.

Yet our investigation involves another requirement: to focus only on those apocalyptic texts which can plausibly be dated prior to or roughly contemporaneous with our New Testament texts. Why? If our goal is to try to understand the form of an apocalyptic text against the backdrop of other texts like it from an ideal first-century hearer's point of view, we are limited historically by the texts we can use to establish that backdrop. In other words, when we hear a knock-knock joke, we can only judge its value as a joke relative to other ones like it that we have heard or that might have influenced the history of the knock-knock joke form.

This is not to say, however, that every flesh-and-blood, first-century hearer of an apocalyptic text like 1 Thessalonians 4:13–18 would have already read or heard any of the relevant Jewish apocalypses listed above. Short of having a video of the first-century Thessalonians unrolling a scroll of the *Apocalypse of Abraham* just before hearing Paul's first letter read to them, it would be well-nigh impossible to prove their awareness.

The limited evidence we have and the formal investigation we propose suggest approaching the problem from the standpoint of an "ideal hearer," the kind of hearer that Paul or the evangelists might have presupposed (consciously or unconsciously) as they wrote. Given that biblical writers could have no knowledge of an apocalyptic text written after their time, limiting ourselves to texts of their day or earlier ones seems, at the very least, prudent and will actually prove productive for our purposes below. So let us turn to a concrete biblical text to see how considerations of form and genre work with a bona fide apocalyptic text.

LET THE HEARER UNDERSTAND:
FORM AND THE APOCALYPTIC THEOPHANY
IN MARK 13:24–37

In applying our understandings of genre and form to Jesus' speech on the Mount of Olives in Mark, we are claiming that Mark is incorporating into his Gospel an apocalyptic form. In fact, in a comparison of one part of this pericope for Advent 1B, Mark 13:24–27, to texts like it in other apocalypses, both similarities and differences become immediately apparent. However, to get the impact of this knock-knock pattern on Mark's ideal hearers, we must first try to discern its form.

[13:24] But in those days after that distress
    "the sun will be darkened,
        and the moon will not give its light,

[25] and the stars will be falling from heaven,
  and the powers in the heavens will be shaken,"
[26] then they will see Humanity's Child coming in the clouds with much power and glory. [27] Then he will send the angels and gather together his chosen ones from the four winds—from the edge of the earth to the edge of heaven. (trans. mine)

The text includes three elements. The first is a description of a cosmos gone awry. The second is the arrival of Humanity's Child (the Son of Man) on the clouds.[14] The third is the angels gathering the elect from all over creation. Formally, Mark's little apocalyptic scene looks like this:

cosmos convulses

+

divine figure arrives

+

angels gather the elect

Although Mark 13:24–27 is associated with the vision in Daniel 7:13–14 (a throne-room vision scene with the Son of Man coming on the clouds), an apocalyptic version of the theophany form stands behind Mark 13:24–27. Why a theophany? Unlike throne-room visions, theophanies feature divine figures coming *and* cosmic convulsions—and typically within an earthly rather than a heavenly throne-room setting. To prove this, we'll need to look at theophanies in the Hebrew Bible and in apocalypses and related literature.

Step 1: Identify Antecedents for the Form in the Hebrew Bible

Many preachers will have already run into numerous theophanic texts in the Hebrew Bible. Some will wish, therefore, to compare those familiar texts with Mark's to begin looking for similarities and differences.

If theophany is not a familiar form, however, preachers may wish to consult two resources that might help their research. The first is a good annotated Bible. Occasionally annotated Bibles will point to other texts with similar wording. Even better, however, are the ample marginal notes in the Nestle-Aland *Novum Testamentum Graece* or the footnotes in the United Bible Societies' *The Greek New Testament*. Such references frequently point to a number of similar texts.

Because of the importance of theophanies in the Hebrew Bible, many scholars have tried to get at the basic features of the theophanic form. In particular, scholars have looked both at (1) what elements theophanies include and (2) the order in which those elements appear.

Why do such things matter? Let's return to our knock-knock joke. As patterned communication the knock-knock joke consistently uses certain elements: two interrogative phrases involving identity (such as "Who's there?"), an indicative disclosure of the door knocker, a punch line, and, of course, the opening "Knock, knock" interjection itself. Looking over the list, however, we note that these five elements of the form are listed out of order. *It takes the right elements in the right order to have a knock-knock joke.* In other words, the elements must be in an expected, sequential order for the knock-knock joke form to function.

A Knock, knock.	(Opening formal signal)
B Who's there?	(Opening interrogative)
C Dwayne.	(Indicative disclosure)
D Dwayne who?	(Second interrogative)
E Dwayne the pool, I'm dwowning!	(Punch line)

Analyzing the elements and order of forms in this way will aid us in learning how the theophanic form works—so we, too, can "get the joke."

In the Hebrew Bible a theophany includes two basic elements in a typical order:

A God speaks, goes, or arrives.
B Nature convulses.

The Hebrew Bible has many such examples of this basic theophanic form:

A *Lord,* when you *went out* from Seir,
      when you *marched* from the region of Edom,
B the *earth trembled,*
      and the *heavens poured,*
      the *clouds* indeed *poured water.*
   The *mountains quaked* before the Lord, the One of Sinai,
      before the Lord, the God of Israel. (Judg. 5:4–5)

This common pattern is also picked up later in prophetic literature:

A The *Lord roars* from Zion,
      and *utters his voice* from Jerusalem;

B the *pastures* of the shepherds *wither,*
 and the top of *Carmel dries up.* (Amos 1:2)

The form can be rather elaborate, especially in "proto-apocalyptic" texts:

A See, the day of the *Lord comes,*
 cruel, with wrath and fierce anger
B to make the *earth a desolation,*
 and to destroy its sinners from it.
 For the *stars of the heavens and their constellations*
 will not give their light;
 the *sun will be dark* at its rising,
 and *the moon will not shed its light.* (Isa. 13:9–10)

While the form can be occasionally inverted and/or expanded (see Joel 2:10–11), the typical order is not only pervasive but persistent.[15] It was, in other words, a common, available, and familiar literary form. As such, these texts show a familiar pattern of communication: God's arrival, sometimes as a mighty warrior, sometimes on the so-called day of the Lord, brings with it cosmic portents.

Step 2: Look for the Form in Jewish Apocalypses

With an idea of what to look for, we next try to see how the theophanic form reappears in apocalypses and related literary types. This is the most difficult part of the task. Most preachers have a good facility with the Bible—even when we cannot quote chapter and verse, we at least know where to look or how to find what we are looking for. Jewish apocalypses, however, are another matter. Most of us are familiar with Daniel 7—12 or Revelation; a few of us may even feel comfortable with *4 Ezra,* which appears in the Apocrypha as 2 Esdras 3—14. However, when it comes to the bulk of the Jewish apocalypses listed earlier, we do not know them well. Preachers may, therefore, need to do some extra work.

 First, we will need to get a copy of noncanonical apocalypses and familiarize ourselves with them. Fortunately, such volumes are often readily available—sometimes even in public libraries.[16] Second, we will want to look for cross-references that help us compare our text to others. Again, an annotated English Bible or, better, a Greek text will offer many leads. Should these not yield enough material, preachers may wish to consult commentaries that make it a point to list noncanonical parallels to biblical texts. The goal is not to be exhaustive but to have a sufficient number of similar texts to compare with our biblical one.

Following the leads that our resources offer, and doing a little reading in this literature on our own, we can find a number of texts that manifest the twofold theophanic form (**A**: the mighty arrival of God; **B**: the reaction of nature). The nine theophanies found in apocalypses are: *1 Enoch* (*Watchers*) 1:3–9; *1 Enoch* 90:18–19 (*Dream Visions*); *1 Enoch* 60:1–6 (*Similitudes*); *Testament of Levi* 3:9–4:1; *4 Ezra* 3:17–19; 5:4–9; 7:33–44; 9:1–9; and 13:1–13.[17] In addition to the ones in apocalypses proper, apocalyptic theophanies also show up in related literary documents prior to the second century C.E.: namely, *Testament of Moses* 10:3–9; *1 Enoch* 91:5b–10 (*Epistle*); *1 Enoch* 102:1–4 (*Epistle*); and a scroll from Qumran, 1QH 3:32–36.[18]

Similarities with Hebrew Bible Theophanies

All of these texts display the twofold form. In what we are calling element **A,** the divine figure typically comes/goes forth or otherwise "looks" (*Testament of Levi* 3:9), is "revealed" (*1 Enoch* 60:2), or speaks thunderously (*1 Enoch* 102:1; 1QH 3:34).[19] In element **B** the cosmos convulses by quaking, trembling, melting, the disruption of heavenly bodies, or the collapse of the natural world.

Not only are both elements present, but the specific order persists in the noncanonical apocalyptic texts cited above. In all of the theophanies, the divine figure's action and the cosmic convulsions are paired every time in Jewish apocalypses and all but one time in related types. While apocalyptic theophanies show some variability in the two formal elements, the **A-B** parts of the theophany's form hold with remarkable tenacity.[20]

A Difference in Apocalyptic Theophanies: Element C and Eschatological Outcomes

What is more interesting about these theophanies, however, is the way they differ from their Hebrew Bible antecedents: the addition of a new element to the theophanic form, which we call element **C**, a description of eschatological outcomes.[21] These eschatological outcomes involve some kind of universal judgment followed by eschatological salvation.

APOCALYPTIC TEXT	ESCHATOLOGICAL SALVATION	ESCHATOLOGICAL JUDGMENT
1 Enoch 1:8–9 (*Watchers*)	peace for the righteous	destruction for the wicked

1 Enoch 90:19 (*Dream Visions*)	execution of judgment by the "sheep"	termination of the "beasts of the field"
1 Enoch 60:6 (*Similitudes*)	covenant for the elect	inquisition for the sinners
Testament of Levi 4:1	—	punishment
4 Ezra 7:36–38	the place of rest/ paradise	appearance of the pit of torment, furnace of hell
4 Ezra 9:7–9	survival of dangers by the saved	dwelling in torments for those who have rejected God's ways
4 Ezra 13:9–13	calling to assembly of the peaceable multitude	destruction by fiery breath for the fighting multitude

The formal element **C** continues with almost the same frequency and dual character in apocalyptic theophanies in "related types":

"RELATED TYPE" TEXT	GOOD NEWS	BAD NEWS
Testament of Moses 10:7b–9	happiness for Israel in starry, heavenly habitations	vengeance on the nations with destruction of their idols
1 Enoch 91:9b–10 (*Epistle*)	cutting off of oppression through the arising of the righteous and wise	judgment fire (for heathen or towers?)
1 Enoch 102:3b–4 (*Epistle*)	hope for souls of the righteous	souls of sinners eternally accursed

Of course, some apocalyptic theophanies lack element **C**: 4 Ezra 5:4–9 and the Qumran text, 1QH 3:32–36. Moreover, some of them also lack either the dual outcome for good and ill (this is not explicit in *1 Enoch* 90:19) or a specifically eschatological outcome (*4 Ezra* 3:19).

In these apocalyptic theophanies one other recurring feature surfaced: the frequent role of angels and the heavenly hosts. While the presence of angelic figures is hardly typical, the way in which they appear *is* somewhat consistent. In *1 Enoch* 1:3–9 the watchers are quivering, presumably in fear.[22] In *1 Enoch* 60:1b (*Similitudes*) the angels are "agitated with great agitation." The angels in *1 Enoch* 102:3 carry out their orders, and then, according to the Ethiopian manuscript, proceed to hide themselves.[23] Finally, in 1QH 3:35 "the heavenly hosts shall cry out," in apparent convulsing harmony with the cosmos, at the sound of God's thunderous voice. Even without the ambiguous evidence from the *Similitudes,* there is a tendency to portray angels as afraid or fearful in apocalyptic theophanies.[24]

Overall, our foray into apocalyptic literature has yielded a very clear and durable form for an apocalyptic theophany.

    A God speaks, goes, or comes forth.
    B Nature convulses.
    C The eschatological outcomes are shown.

In short, what we have is a knock-knock type of pattern to help us get how the form works. As we shall see, all of these formal features are helpful in establishing a horizon of expectation for hearing Mark 13:24–37 anew.

Step 3: Compare the Apocalyptic Theophany Form with Your Text

We have traced a history of theophany from the Hebrew Bible to Jewish apocalypses, arguing that its **A-B** pattern (divine figure comes/goes/speaks + cosmic convulsions) was enlarged into an **A-B-C** pattern (divine figure comes/goes/speaks + cosmic convulsions + eschatological good news and bad news). We now will argue that this formal pattern appears also in part of our Advent 1B lectionary text, Mark 13:24–27.

Similarities to Apocalyptic Theophanies

Using the features described above as consistent elements of the apocalyptic theophany form, we come to the following conclusions about Mark's appropriation of it. First, Mark sets up the theophany with many of the typical elements: the coming of a divine figure, the accompanying cosmic convulsions, and an eschatological outcome of judgment and/or salvation. In the translation below the presence of all three elements becomes clear.

A God speaks, goes, or comes forth.	But in those days after that distress "*the sun will be darkened, and the moon will not give its light, and the stars*

		will be falling from heaven, and the powers in the heavens will be shaken," then they will see
B	*Nature convulses.*	**Humanity's Child coming in the clouds with much power and glory.** *Then he will send the angels and gather together his chosen ones*
C	*Eschatological outcomes are shown.*	*from the four winds—from the edge of the earth to the edge of heaven.*

Differences in Mark's Apocalyptic Theophany

Inversion of Order

The first thing we notice is Mark's inversion of the formal order. While other apocalyptic theophanies have done the same (esp. *1 Enoch* 60:1–6 [*Similitudes*]), the fact that Mark varies the typical order is significant. Mark's inversion heightens the hearers' sense that God's coming is imminent.

Change in Protagonist

Who appears when element **A** finally comes into play? Humanity's Child, the Son of Man. In other apocalyptic theophanies there was some variation as to the divine title of the One coming/going forth/speaking in element **A**.[25] With the *possible* exception of *4 Ezra*, there is, however, no formal precedent for an apocalyptic theophany presided over by another mediator. Doubtless Mark is drawing on a common "type scene" here. He describes Humanity's Child as coming with "great power and glory," powerful divine attributes. Mark's use of the form keeps forcing hearers to revise their expectations about how apocalyptic theophanies happen, who presides over them, and, as we shall see, what their eschatological outcomes are.

A Uniquely Salvific Eschatological Outcome

With element **C** in Mark 13:27 the form's subversion continues apace. Mark's apocalyptic theophany may have inverted elements **B** and **A**, but he at least gives us element **C** in good order. Or does he? We recall that apocalyptic theophanies start typically with God's coming/going forth, proceed to cosmic convulsions, and then close with universal judgment and dual eschatological outcomes for sinners and the elect. With Mark 13:27, however, that expectation is subverted. Not only is there no universal judgment connected with it, but the only eschatological outcome sketched is that of the chosen ones being gathered.

Angels Don't Fear, but Aid
in Eschatological Salvation

And who conducts this gathering? Angels! The very ones who in the apocalyptic theophany typically cringe in fear now act at the behest of Humanity's Child (Son of Man) to collect the elect "from the four winds—from the edge of the earth to the edge of heaven."

To summarize, while the generic features in the theophany text raise the expectation of a judgment scene, Mark's apocalyptic theophany unexpectedly transforms judgment into universal eschatological salvation.[26] In this respect Mark both meets and subverts the expectations generated by its formal precedents in Jewish apocalypses.[27] Moreover, for Mark the apocalyptic theophany has become a revelation of Humanity's Child, the Son of Man.

Step 4: Determine the Significance
of the Text's Use of the Form

What does it mean for our formal analysis that the apocalyptic theophany appears as it does in Mark 13:24–37? First, for the Markan hearers the cosmic future comes with the advent of Humanity's Child (13:26), who is mentioned frequently throughout Mark's Gospel (2:10, 28; 8:31, 38; 9:9, 12, 31; 10:33, 45; 14:21, 41, and 62). It is precisely Humanity's Child who will die (8:31; 9:12, 31; 10:33 and 45) and who stands at the head of the glorious theophanic vision (13:26; see also the anticipated glory in 8:38 and 14:62). The cumulative rhetorical effect of associating Humanity's Child with death and glory throughout Mark's Gospel forces a complete revision about expectations of God's end-time dealings.

Second, we recall that the fear of the apocalyptic theophany is universal, including even angels in many earlier apocalyptic theophanies.[28] Yet in Mark's text the fearful reaction of angels and/or all humanity has disappeared. This represents a significant departure from the apocalyptic theophany—one which would have been heard loud and clear.[29] Indeed the fearless expectation generated by Mark's apocalyptic form is confirmed by what follows. The cursed fig tree of Mark 11 is now the locus of a salvific sign in 13:28: "From the fig tree learn the parable—when its branch becomes tender and shoots shoots, know that summer is near!" The typical expectation of fear, a standard element of the apocalyptic theophany, has been transfigured into expectant hope.[30]

Third, and most important in Mark's apocalyptic form, eschatological salvation no longer follows its counterparts of judgment and wrath. Mark has turned the typical order of universal judgment and blessing for the elect in the apocalyptic theophanies on its head. Again, the value of the subversion of this typical generic feature would not be lost on hearers who share its conventions.

Form of Text and Form of Sermon

The strategic use of form in Mark 13:24–27 has given us many helpful cues for how we might structure our sermon. Initially, the form plays on an expectation of judgment. Mark's depiction of cosmic convulsions heightens dread. Thus, setting up the form's starting point should be no problem at all. However, a sermon should make a move to Mark's formal inversion. The future we so often dread is really about the New Thing—the salvation that God is doing in Jesus Christ. Knock, knock! Who's there? Jesus, the merciful One, the Gatherer, the One who brings not fear but salvation.

---

1. James L. Bailey, "Genre Analysis," in *Hearing the New Testament: Strategies for Interpretation,* ed. Joel B. Green (Grand Rapids: Eerdmans, 1995), 200.

2. Thomas G. Long, *The Witness of Preaching* (Louisville, Ky.: Westminster/John Knox, 1989), 92–93. Long writes elsewhere about some homiletical possibilities offered by particular literary forms in the scriptures (*Preaching and the Literary Forms of the Bible* [Philadelphia: Fortress, 1989]).

3. Consider, e.g., Micah 6:1–8 from the perspective of form criticism. On the surface the text looks like just another prophetic oracle. Yet on closer, formal inspection form critics see elements of a covenant lawsuit (Hebrew: *rîb*). The summoning of witnesses in 6:1–2, the review of evidence in 6:3–5, and the contrition of the guilty in 6:6–7 point to this form's origin in a setting of justice at the city gate. Armed with this information, form critics can then speculate that Micah 6:1–8 has a prior oral history in a certain life-setting (a public court of some kind), which then in turn sheds light on the form's function in that setting.

    While information about a community can be valuable and interesting, it sometimes yields little for the preacher. Assuming, for a moment, with the form critics that forms are traceable to certain historical life-settings, what are we to do with the same text in a different life-setting like ours? Part of the problem is that the form critic, in focusing exclusively on an ancient community behind a text, fails to help the preacher discern how this form might function in a contemporary community.

    Perhaps, then, we need to view the issues of form and function not so much in terms of communities that produce them but in terms of hearers who would hear them. One of the early distinctive marks of form criticism is its assumption that behind a written text stands an oral history. What, however, if we were to take the fundamental orality of forms seriously enough to consider how they function in relation to communities as hearers in front of the words, and not just view the same hearers as institutional producers of oral forms behind the words?

    If we return to Micah 6:1–8 using this point of view, the issues of form look different. Rather than focusing solely on the covenant lawsuit (*rîb*) form as it relates to prior institutions in the life of historical Israel, we might try relating the form to the hearers for whom it is destined: God's people. In this case, the covenant lawsuit is telling, not as a typical manifestation of oral, institutional life, but as a strikingly unusual, corporate indictment of Israel's life in the presence of God. With a simple change of orientation, the form suddenly comes alive and becomes eminently preachable.

4. The language of the sermon introduction as promise comes from Thomas G. Long (*Witness,* 138ff.). The psychotherapeutic "contract" metaphor, which seems to imply something of a more explicit disclosure, emerges in the pastoral-communicational contribution of J. Randall Nichols (*Building the Word: The Dynamics of Communication and Preaching* [San Francisco: Harper & Row, 1960], 101). A perhaps further extreme would be represented by the Toastmasters' public-speaking shibboleth on introductions and speeches: "Tell 'em what you're gonna say, say it, and then tell 'em what you told 'em!" Because of the importance in establishing a delayed disclosure of meaning in the sermon, many homileticians argue against disclosing too much in the introduction, frequently likening it to showing your cards at a poker table. Regardless of how little or how much is said in an introduction, however, something of a horizon of expectation is established from the hearers' point of view.

5. Eugene Lowry attempts to combine in his "homiletical plot" a classically liberal theological perspective that views itself as "continuous" with human experience and a more Barthian one that is "discontinuous" with the same (*The Homiletical Plot* [Atlanta: John Knox, 1980], 65f.). Clearly behind these and other issues of "form" are profoundly theological matters of gospel. Does the gospel emerge out of our "horizon of expectation" or what we know by virtue of participating in creation? Or does the gospel negate all that together with human constructions of "religion" and/or culture? Preachers need to be aware that such choices about form are never merely technical or purely aesthetic, but profoundly theological.

6. Karl Barth, *Homiletics,* trans. Geoffrey Bromiley and Donald E. Daniels (Louisville, Ky.: Westminster/John Knox, 1991), 121–25.

7. The proper generic designation for the four Gospels is a matter of some scholarly dispute. Are they like biographies, akin to romance novels, or a *genre sui generis,* that is, a genre unto themselves? Whatever genre they are, they do seem suitable for grouping together. For a helpful discussion of the problem, see Mary Ann Tolbert, *Sowing the Gospel: Mark's World in Literary-Historical Perspective* (Minneapolis: Fortress, 1989), 48–79.

8. The term "type scene" is being used in the sense that Robert Alter established in his study of literary conventions in the Hebrew Bible (*The Art of Biblical Narrative* [New York: Basic, 1981], 47–62).

9. As we begin to look at matters of genre and form in apocalyptic texts, we must first confess the obvious: there is no ancient literary guide that defines the forms of apocalyptic texts. Why? For one thing the apocalypse is not exactly a genre that belongs to high literature. Apocalyptic texts, like most other biblical texts, were and are not products of elite literary circles. Indeed, as Bible scholar Mary Ann Tolbert notes about the Gospel of Mark, they are more like "popular literature" (*Sowing the Gospel: Mark's World in Literary-Historical Perspective* [Minneapolis: Fortress, 1989], 70ff.). What Tolbert applies to her reading of Mark, we are applying by extension to other New Testament texts. For her, popular literature is distinguished from elite literature, which is written for the highly educated, *and* folktales, which are more "local and tribal in compass."

The problem then becomes this: How do you define apocalyptic forms if no ancient writer attained any level of high literary self-consciousness to do so? How can we name a form that its ancient producers themselves never recognized? Naturally, we cannot do so without a sober sense that we could be wrong. Yet there is one thing we can do. We can base our literary conclusions on careful readings of *extant* apocalypses. While we do not have Aristotle's *Apocalyptic Poetics* or Longinus's *On the Sublime Apocalypse,* we do have lots of canonical and noncanonical writings like our apocalyptic texts in the New Testament. These will need to form the baseline for our critical judgments about forms of apocalyptic texts.

10. As a result of the Apocalypse Group's careful research of the genre, we will use their list of Jewish apocalypses as a generic baseline for comparing apocalyptic forms in the New Testament: Daniel 7—12, *The Animal Apocalypse* (*1 Enoch* 85—90), *The Apocalypse of Weeks* (*1 Enoch* 93; 91:12–17), *Jubilees* 23, *4 Ezra* (also known from the Apocrypha as *2 Esdras* 3—14), *2 Baruch, The Apocalypse of Abraham, The Book of the Watchers* (*1 Enoch* 1—36), *The Book of the Heavenly Luminaries* (*1 Enoch* 72—82), *The Similitudes of Enoch* (*1 Enoch* 37—71), *2 Enoch, Testament of Levi* 2—5, *3 Baruch, The Testament of Abraham* 10—15, and *The Apocalypse of Zephaniah.*

11. This rather arbitrary date is chosen because most New Testament texts were committed to writing in the second half of the first century, or possibly into the early second. Given the fact that many writings, both noncanonical and canonical, likely had some sort of oral or fragmentary literary history behind the versions we have now, their value for such a formal reconstruction can make no claims to hard, scientific truth, but rather is itself the result of considered literary-critical judgments.

12. From the provenance of apocalyptic writings, it is clear that Jews both in and out of the Diaspora were producing apocalyptic writings. For the apocalypses and their varying provenances, see the introductions to the various writings in James Charlesworth's edited collection (*The Old Testament Pseudepigrapha: Apocalyptic Literature and Testaments,* vol. 1 [New York: Doubleday, 1983]). Another piece of evidence that buttresses the claim of broad appeal is the great variety of languages in which many of these apocalypses appear: Greek, Latin, Aramaic, Ge'ez, etc. Whether in original volumes or subsequent translations, Jewish apocalypses clearly had a broad circulation in a variety of contexts.

13. John J. Collins, "Jewish Apocalyptic against Its Hellenistic Near Eastern Environment," *Bulletin of the American Schools of Oriental Research* 220 [1975]: 27–36.

14. See chap. 2, n. 18, for an explanation of my use of "Humanity's Child" for the traditional designation "Son of Man."

15. Jörg Jeremias: "This pattern is documented in the oldest poetry of Israel . . . *and was still in use in post-OT times*" (emphasis mine). "Theophany in the OT," *Interpreter's Dictionary of the Bible Supplementary Volume* (Nashville: Abingdon, 1962), 897.

16. A good, recent edition is that of Charlesworth's *Old Testament Pseudepigrapha.* This volume is especially useful for research because of its cross-references to scriptural texts and its introductions to the individual apocalypses and related writings. It may be the most thorough and up-to-date edition available (compare H. F. D. Sparks, ed., *The Apocryphal Old Testament* [Oxford: Clarendon,

1984]). Those wishing to find a cheaper paperback edition may wish to turn to that of Mitchell Reddish, *Apocalyptic Literature* (Nashville: Hendrickson, 1990). The translations are the same as those in Charlesworth's edition but do not come with its extensive annotations and other research helps.

17. Following John Collins and the Society of Biblical Literature's Apocalypse Group, all the above fall into the definition of the genre, including *Testament of Levi* 2—5, which represents an apocalypse embedded in a testament ("The Jewish Apocalypses," *Semeia* 14 [1979]: 29–44). While the texts (excepting *Testament of Levi*) are listed in the order of the dates assigned by Collins, the dating of the above apocalypses prior to 100 C.E. is not without its pitfalls. The most controversial of these are likely the passages from the *Similitudes* and *Testament of Levi*. Although most scholars date the *Similitudes* to the first century C.E., or possibly B.C.E. (E. Isaac, "1 Enoch," in *The Old Testament Pseudepigrapha* 1.7; Matthew Black, *The Book of Enoch or 1 Enoch* [Leiden: Brill, 1985], 188), some do argue for a much later dating of the *Similitudes* (see Jozef T. Milik, *The Books of Enoch* [Oxford: Clarendon, 1976], 91–96). Even more uncertain is the dating of *Testament of Levi,* which, together with other parts of *Testament of the Twelve Patriarchs,* is dated as early as the second century B.C.E. and as late as 200 C.E. (Collins, "Jewish Apocalypses," 46). Yet even if *Testament of Levi* is to be dated later, that only demonstrates the vitality of the form we are studying in apocalypses. At any rate, the problem of dating these texts does not loom large for the kind of genre analysis we undertake here. First, unlike tradition-historical studies, our analysis does not require that we know the exact chronological progression of the literary exemplars. It is enough to know that they are likely prior to or roughly contemporaneous with our New Testament text (hence the choice of 100 C.E. as an upper cutoff point) so that we can embed it in an appropriate generic matrix. Second, the problems of dating these documents themselves are in part a result of frequent Christian redactions of Jewish writings. For our purposes, however, the question is not whether the documents are Jewish or Christian redactions (how can we so easily separate the two in the first century C.E.?) but whether such provenance would force us to date them after 100 C.E. (for example, a first-century B.C.E. Christian apocalyptic form should be an oxymoron!).

18. With the exception of the Qumran *Hodayot,* all of the above examples come from testaments, two of them embedded in the Enoch literature. As with the apocalypses cited earlier, questions of dating are problematic. Nonetheless, it is relatively safe to say that our texts can be dated before our required 100 C.E. cutoff (Collins, "Jewish Apocalypses," 44–49).

19. These variations on the form are explained in Jörg Jeremias's delineation of the history of the theophany (*Theophanie: Die Geschichte einer alttestamentlichen Gattung* [Neukirchen-Vluyn: Neukirchener Verlag, 1977], 16–24). Over the course of time Yahweh's voice (Amos 1:2; Ps. 76:9), glance (Ps. 104:32), or manifestation as king (Ps. 99:1) was likewise coupled with natural convulsions. Some of these are also occasionally attested in nonapocalyptic literature of early Judaism (Sir. 43:17a, 16a).

20. When element **A** appears first, element **B** follows immediately in 87 percent of Jewish apocalypses, 67 percent in the related types, and 80 percent of apocalyptic theophanies overall. When element **B** occurs first, it is followed immediately by element **A** in every case.

21. In his comparison of *1 Enoch* 1:3–9 and *Testament of Moses* 10, Lars Hartman argues that eschatological blessing and judgment are constituent features of the apocalyptic theophany (*Asking for a Meaning* [Lund: CWK Gleerup, 1979], 24–26, 48). Claus Westermann's epiphany form includes a third element, "God's wrathful intervention for or against" (*The Praise of God in the Psalms* [Richmond: John Knox, 1965], 98). While Westermann has a difficult time finding sufficient exemplars to buttress his formal claims, a third such element in an eschatological mode does seem present in our noncanonical apocalyptic texts.

22. The "holy ones" sharing in executing judgment in 1:9 are not explicitly angels.

23. While I am loathe to advocate a reading of 102:3 that is not well supported in scholarly circles, the more difficult reading of the Ethiopian manuscript supports our trend, albeit teasingly (Black, *Book of Enoch,* 311).

24. Compare *1 Enoch* 60:4–5, where the individual angel Michael performs the typically apocalyptic function of angelic interpreter of heavenly events. Nonetheless, this different function of the angel Michael (in a way consonant with the genre apocalypse) does not negate the typical role of the "angels" as fearful in our apocalyptic theophanies. Jeremias (*Theophanie,* 52) has also noticed the typicality of this angelic role in *1 Enoch* 1:3–9. Jeremias sees this as an expansion upon the motif of human fear in Hebrew Bible theophanies.

25. The titles are: the God of the Universe (*1 Enoch* 1:3 [*Watchers*]), the Lord of the Sheep (*1 Enoch* 90:18 [*Dream Visions*]), the Antecedent of Time (*1 Enoch* 60:2 [*Similitudes*]), the Lord (*Testament of Levi* 3:9), Sovereign Lord (implied in *4 Ezra* 3:17), one whom the many do not know (*4 Ezra* 5:7b), the Most High (*4 Ezra* 7:33; 9:2; implied in *1 Enoch* 102:1 [*Epistle*]), the Man from the Sea (*4 Ezra* 13:3), the Heavenly One (*Testament of Moses* 10:3), and the holy Lord (*1 Enoch* 91:7c [*Epistle*]).

26. Such an odd subversion of the form squares with our rhetorical analysis in chap. 2. We recall that parenesis switches from positive to negative forms before and after the apocalyptic theophany of Mark 13:24–27. Perhaps Mark's apocalyptic theophany without universal judgment is designed to help reorient the kind of watching which Jesus calls for—not a watching out for fearful signs (they can mislead), but a watching for salvation.

27. This study is not the first to suggest that Mark engages in a rhetoric of indirection with his hearers. Robert Fowler investigates something similar (*Let the Reader Understand: Reader-Response Criticism and the Gospel of Mark* [Minneapolis: Fortress, 1991], 155–94).

28. In addition to the trembling of the cosmic convulsions in element **B**, human beings are also typically fearful of apocalyptic theophanies. See *1 Enoch* 1:4b–5 (*Watchers*); *1 Enoch* 90:19c (implied) (*Epistle*); *1 Enoch* 60:3 (*Similitudes*); *Testament of Levi* 3:9b; *4 Ezra* 5:5; 9:3; 13:4, 8; *Testament of Moses* 10:4 (implied); *1 Enoch* 102:1 (*Epistle*); and 1QH 3:33 ("rave").

29. Hartman argues that the Sinai theophany represents a "topos" common in postbiblical Jewish texts (*Asking,* 42).

30. Beyond our limited genre analysis several other literary features also tie and integrate Mark 13 into the literary context of the entire Markan Gospel. Mary Ann Tolbert (*Sowing the Gospel,* 257) has noted that prior to and directly following the speech the reliability of Jesus' word is established through the fulfillment of his predictions (Mark 11:2–6; 14:13–16). Yet Tolbert also notes

(*Sowing*, 259) that Jesus' companions at this point tie this episode closely to the Gethsemane episode (14:32–52). Indeed, the verb "watch" itself (along with several other catchwords) plays a prominent role in both. Another telling literary feature can be seen in the figure of the fig tree. In Mark 11:12–14 Jesus curses the fig tree. In Mark 11:20–25 Jesus uses the withered fig tree as an example. Surprisingly, here in vv. 28–29 Jesus uses the budding fig tree as a figure of salvation! Yet perhaps the greatest literary element to consider with reference to our text is its location. The speech occurs on the Mount of Olives opposite the Temple. The great split between Jesus and the authorities is in the open. Now Jesus' speech is given from a place of judgment. D. E. Nineham notes: "The mountain was the traditional place of revelation, and compare Zechariah 14:4 for the Mount of Olives in particular (v. 3) as the destined scene of the apocalyptic judgment" (*The Gospel of St. Mark* [Harmondsworth, Middlesex: Penguin, 1963], 342). Here the scene for our speech is set in such a way as to awaken the expectation of judgment. Thus, from a literary-critical perspective our text is crucial in modifying that tradition within the context of Jesus' apocalyptic discourse in addition to linking the Gethsemane story to the discourse's emphasis on the praxis of watching. Indeed, even this brief review of the literary-critical context reveals the important connections of the apocalyptic discourse to the entire Gospel of Mark.

Chapter 4

What in the World We Will See along the Way: Reading Cosmic Apocalyptic Signs and Symbols

In 1994 one of the many first-time Republican congressional winners was shocked at the margin of victory he and his party had at the polls. In fact, he was so surprised, he designated this seismic shift in the electorate an "earthquake." The next day the local Democratic-leaning daily picked up his quote in an editorial cartoon of a donkey, covered up to its neck in rubble, speaking sarcastically to the same Republican candidate: "The proper term is *landslide,* rookie" (emphasis mine).[1]

For our purposes the two above attempts at using symbolic language to speak about massive social and political change are telling. The first was a new congressman's attempt to make sense of a seismic shift in the electorate. While it was not the typical, hackneyed response (the "landslide" electoral victory), by his unique choice of metaphor he demonstrated how we often grope for meaning in times of massive social change. We rely upon cosmic, symbolic language. Yet the very fact that the newspaper editorial cartoonist answered with the more traditional metaphor of "landslide" indicates that such use of cosmic symbolic language is more common than we think.

In this chapter we will look at the cosmic symbolic language of apocalyptic texts in the same sort of way. We will try to show how apocalyptic symbols in the New Testament are attempts at negotiating a *social world*. By the end of the chapter, though, we'll see that such a social reading of the highly charged cosmic symbols in apocalyptic texts makes sense of both apocalypses and our contemporary world.

THE PROBLEM: SYMBOLIC LANGUAGE IN THE AGE OF SCIENCE AND THERAPY

Imagine you have a couple of guests over for coffee in your home, say, Karl Marx and Sigmund Freud (Friedrich Nietzsche was sick and couldn't come). You know how it goes: just a couple of imaginary intellectual giants sipping java with you.

During a lull in the conversation, you, Marx, and Freud pause to look at a painting from the book *The Gospel in Art by the Peasants of Solentiname,* which lies open on the coffee table between you. The painting depicts Luke's crucifixion scene with Nicaraguan peasant women bearing flowers surrounding Christ, who is portrayed as a Central American peasant, dying on the cross.[2]

After contemplating this work of art, you and your two guests find yourselves discussing it. "Clearly the picture is about the triumph of the Superego over the Ego," offers Sigmund Freud. "The peasant Jesus surrenders everything to the Father, while the women look on adoringly at the cross, which is also a phallic symbol." "Nein, nein!" Karl Marx chimes in, "That's just psychobabble, Sigmund. Religion is the opiate of the people! The women show gratitude for Christ's sacrificial death, as a way of drawing attention away from the concrete need for class struggle."[3]

Such an imaginary situation seems extraordinary to us. Yet the course of their discussion is strangely familiar. It seems we're always stuck with the same old split that troubles Sigmund and Karl at the Kaffeeklatsch: we tend to assume that symbols either describe something "out there" or express something "in here." For us moderns, symbols refer to either objective reality or interior subjectivity.

SYMBOLIC LANGUAGE AND OBJECTIVE REFERENCE

The objective side of the split is hardly new in the history of interpretation of apocalyptic symbols. On the level of popular interpretation, apocalyptic symbols of cosmic scope have long had a powerful hold on contemporary imagination. Many historians have traced how various groups at various times and places have taken such symbolic language quite literally—in other words, as referring to a reality "out there." Most recently, as Elisabeth

Schüssler Fiorenza points out, some right-wing religious groups have tried to set up apocalyptic timetables based on a "correspondence of terms" approach to Revelation.[4] Such a literalistic reading "understands Revelation's symbolic language as divinely coded language and claims that it has found the only way to transcribe it into referential propositional language."[5]

In fairness, however, it is important to note that referential views of apocalyptic symbols are not solely the province of millennial groups. Indeed, many modern historical approaches have done something similar. The millennialist assumes a one-to-one correspondence between world historical events, whether present or future, and the symbolic language of apocalyptic texts (for example, the prediction of plagues in Rev. 9:13–21 = AIDS). The thoroughgoing historian assumes that an apocalyptic symbol has a single real-world referent within its text's own time frame. Thus, some historians may try to figure out how cosmic symbols such as plagues or falling stars correspond to actual, contemporaneous historical events like epidemics or astral phenomena around the end of the first century C.E.

Naturally the impulse behind such an objective, referential reading of apocalyptic symbols is good. Under the influence of Enlightenment rationality, the historian assumes that language has a generally referential purpose within its own context. By decoding the symbolic language of apocalyptic texts within their own historical frames of reference (rather than in a contemporary one), the historian can establish a plausible meaning consistent with other historical evidence. The influence and import of such a scientific approach to exegesis is not to be underestimated. Such careful reconstructions of history give texture to the biblical texts we use for preaching.

So when are referential readings of apocalyptic symbols helpful and when not? Perhaps we can make the strengths and limitations of referential approaches to the symbolic language of apocalypses clearer with an example from the Bible. Consider this text from Daniel's vision:

In the first year of King Belshazzar of Babylon, Daniel had a dream and visions of his head as he lay in bed. Then he wrote down the dream: I, Daniel, saw in my vision by night the four winds of heaven stirring up the great sea, and four great beasts came up out of the sea, different from one another. The first was like a lion and had eagles' wings. Then, as I watched, its wings were plucked off, and it was lifted up from the ground and made to stand on two feet like a human being; and a human mind was given to it. Another beast appeared, a second one, that looked like a bear. It was raised up on one side, had three tusks in its mouth among its teeth and was told, "Arise, devour many bodies!" After this, as I watched, another appeared, like a leopard. The beast had four wings of a bird on its back and four heads; and dominion was given to it. After this I saw in the visions by night a fourth beast, terrifying and dreadful and exceedingly strong. It had great iron teeth and was devouring, breaking in pieces, and stamping what was left with its feet. It was different from all the beasts that had preceded it, and it had ten horns. I was considering the horns, when another horn appeared, a little one coming up among them; to make room for it, three of the earlier horns were plucked up by the roots. There were eyes like human eyes in this horn, and a mouth speaking arrogantly. (Dan. 7:1–8)

What shall we make of Daniel's symbolic language? A contemporary millennialist would, of course, try to link these four beasts to contemporary phenomena, say, succeeding "evil empires" of recent history. Perhaps the first beast would be the Nazis; the second, the Russians; the third, the Chinese; and now in this end of all ages the final and most terrible of beasts, the dreaded empire of . . . (the reader fills in the blank).

Since this obviously anachronistic use of Daniel's symbolic language is problematic, scientific exegesis offers an alternative set of correspondences. The annotation to this particular text in the NRSV offers a fine example of the historical-critical consensus:

The winged lion represents the Babylonian empire, the bear the Medes, the four-headed winged leopard the Persians, the dragon-like beast the Greeks, whose ten horns represent the ten rulers who succeeded Alexander. The *little* horn (compare 8.9) is Antiochus Epiphanes, who gained his throne by uprooting others.[6]

Nonetheless, even the best attempts to discover clear historical referents for apocalyptic symbols run into intractable problems. In fact, apocalyptic symbols often seem to *resist* such reductions—even historical-critical ones.[7] For example, while in a cursory reading the four beasts lend themselves quite easily to a historical periodization of Israel's imperial overlords over time, a careful examination of the evidence reveals some difficulties. Concerning the fourth beast's eleventh "little horn," for example, commentator W. Sibley Towner writes,

This verse obviously is a crucial one, then, for identifying the actual historical setting in which the book of Daniel was written, because it is given to Daniel to witness the demise of this particular eleventh post-Alexandrian king and no other. *Whether Antiochus IV Epiphanes was actually the eleventh king in this sequence of monarchs is open to considerable question,* though one way of counting produces just such a number. (emphasis mine)[8]

Norman Porteous, who tries to figure out the identity of the three "up-rooted" horns, disputes that the eleventh horn's identity is ambiguous, even while echoing a similar thought about determining exact correspondences:

> There is no doubt at all that he [Antiochus IV Epiphanes] is the small horn springing up among the other horns, to make room for which three horns are rooted out. There has been endless discussion as to the identity of these horns and perhaps it does not greatly matter whom they represent. . . . *Quot homines tot sententiae!* [There are as many opinions as there are people.][9]

The point is not just that historical critics work on the basis of evidence and probabilities. That is the nature of the historian's task. Neither is it important that two critics disagree about a historical referent for a given apocalyptic symbol. What is crucial to interpretation is the propensity of apocalyptic symbols to resist having their meaning *exhausted* by even those historical referents that seem most obvious.[10] We have seen it above with Daniel 7. Precisely at the point when one thinks a certain historical context offers a perfect one-to-one fit between symbol and referent, there is something more to the apocalyptic symbol that refuses to be tied down.

How can this be? Paul Ricoeur offers two intriguing suggestions. First, Ricoeur argues that it is the nature of apocalypses to reduce historical situations, even their own, to types. Daniel purports to receive his vision in Daniel 7:1 during the first year of Babylonian King Belshazzar's reign. Yet Daniel 7 relates his vision to people struggling to be faithful under the heels of Hellenizers like Antiochus Epiphanes, who lived *centuries* after his Babylonian counterpart.[11] The message is clear: from empire to empire, the enemy of the faithful is the same. Or, as writer Kurt Tucholsky puts it:

> Republiken oder Kaiserreiche,
> 's ist immer das gleiche, immer das gleiche!
> [Whether republic or empire's the name,
> it's always the same, always the same.][12]

The apocalypse sets out situations, even its own, in relation to others. Thus Daniel's apocalyptic vision, while arising out of a particular historical context, also invites its readers to transcend that context analogically.

The very functioning of meaning in apocalyptic literature pushes the exegete in this direction. We have seen how the author proceeds to a fictional transference of his heroes into another time in order to express the spirit of resistance to the present persecution, that of Antiochus Epiphanes. In so doing, the author constitutes the past as the model for his own time and prophecy *post eventum* is transformed according to a schematic rule into new prophecy. He has therefore reduced his time and the past to their respective singularity in order to apprehend them as types of situations. The establishment of an analogical relation between one situation and the other thus underlies the very operation of apocalyptic discourse.[13]

Second, Ricoeur actually embraces that which confounds historically minded readers. Many would consider that which cannot be nailed down to a single referent to be a historical loose end. Yet this "loose end" actually invites the reader to participate in the apocalyptic symbol's intrinsic allusiveness (and elusiveness!):

Interpretation here seems to fix upon the identification of individual personages and unique historical situations. In fact, all the energy of some exegetes seems to be given over to a term by term and detail by detail translation: for this beast, this empire; for that horn, that petty king! . . . And yet, even in the case of those figures calling for an unequivocal decipherment, the very fact that the discourse remains *allusive* leaves a margin of free play. The author seems to be saying, "Understand, the beasts are empires and their horns are kings, but guess their names!" The symbolic expansion here finds a narrow piece of manoeuvring room.[14]

Just at the very point where biblical critics wish to focus on the uniqueness of the apocalyptic symbol's setting in life and its transparency to history, the very nature of apocalyptic discourse itself invites readers to look at situations analogically and offers symbols that can be neither domesticated nor comfortably reduced to a single, obvious historical referent.[15] As a result, though historical readings of these symbols shed considerable light, the text itself invites us further, offering us not just the symbolic world behind the text, but another *symbolic* or *social world* in front of it. This world's logic is not that of the historian, who assumes the uniqueness of every historical moment. Rather, this social world's logic is that of the seer, who through situational analogy and symbolic allusiveness draws readers into the interpretive task. In other words, the *function* of these apocalyptic symbols is not just to offer windows to their world of origin, but to invite readers to reread their own world.

At the beginning of this book we considered the stained-glass window of John's heavenly city. In a sense this "symbol" points to the world that begot it. The symbol "new Jerusalem" has a meaning, and it provokes a longing that many of us understand only derivatively—since we were not present when exiles were carted off from Jerusalem to Babylon in the sixth century B.C.E. Nor were we present, by virtue of the analogy in John's time, when Jerusalem was destroyed by the Romans centuries later. Yet the quality of apocalyptic language often nudges us, invites us, and sometimes even startles us out of the historian's backward gaze. Like the stained-glass window of the heavenly city, the symbol also points *forward* and invites us to look at our world through its symbolic vision. Therefore, a search for the definitive historical referents for apocalyptic symbols can only be a beginning step. The symbols of that world also invite us to view our own world in a new light.

APOCALYPTIC SYMBOLS AND
CONTEMPORARY SUBJECTIVITY

The limitations of a purely historical, referential reading of apocalyptic language push our discussion now to a different realm. We have seen that apocalyptic symbols are often not fully transparent to their context, but invite interpretation. The great New Testament scholar Rudolf Bultmann grasped this problem and offered a uniquely modern solution. Bultmann suggested that we must *translate* symbolic language from its ancient worldview.

In broad terms Bultmann is no doubt partly correct. When preachers are confronted with a Sunday lection that treats miracles and ancient three-storied cosmologies of firmament, earth, and Sheol—let alone blood-red moons—they come face to face with Bultmann's hermeneutical problem. So when Bultmann talks about being troubled by ancient worldviews in interpreting biblical texts, those who deal with biblical texts week in and week out can nod their heads in agreement.

Bultmann's solution to this hermeneutical problem is twofold. First, he calls for "demythologization," a method of interpretation that would relieve apocalyptic texts of their mythological baggage and make them intelligible to our modern, scientific world. Yet even a mythically sanitized ancient text is not the final product of the Bultmannian project. In fact, a symbol's translation into our modern world requires a subsequent "re-mythologization" into the categories of existentialist philosophy. Texts with highly charged symbols are interpreted in light of how I understand myself. Mythic symbolic language is really about the interpreter.

For the preacher such a translation of mythological language is important. Ancient texts operating out of a defunct worldview cannot provide understanding on their own terms, but they still can furnish what Bultmann calls symbols, images, and analogies for God's action. Yet any use of such symbolic language always requires Bultmann's Lutheran caveat: this language about God may not be merely conceptual language, but must always be *pro me,* for me.

In the end, though, Bultmann's focus proves too narrow for our cosmic apocalyptic symbols. While Bultmann's desire to translate is helpful, there is more than the mythological equivalent of navel gazing in New Testament apocalyptic texts. If the rest of the scriptural witness as a whole is any indication, the gospel is not just for individuals, but a word of God's love for the world. Indeed, direct address in the New Testament is mostly in the second person plural and less frequently seems bent on addressing rugged, future-projecting individualists.[16]

For that matter, there is also more to *preaching* than assuming our hearers inhabit only the narcissistic pew of our cultural mind. In other words, we don't just preach to individuals; we preach to a community of faith which is itself shaped by powerful social forces. In fact, pushing Bultmann further, the gospel is more than just *pro me* (for me); it is *pro nobis* (for *us*). Perhaps apocalyptic symbols are pushing us beyond our purely individualistic conceptions of faith as well. If so, the problem may be that we who would interpret symbols have done so from split minds: either as hard-headed, cold-hearted historical objectivists who never met a symbol we couldn't find a referent for, or as soft-headed, warm-hearted intrapersonal subjectivists who view every symbol as an extension of our interior lives.

READING SYMBOLS IN A SOCIAL WORLD

Fortunately the tension we experience when we try to interpret cosmic symbols *either* objectively *or* subjectively may well prove to be productive for us. Such a split actually represents a false choice—if we consider symbolic language as speaking to our intersubjective reality, our social world. Perhaps cosmic symbols are neither merely about objective things "out there" nor about subjective things "in here," but about things we share with others—our social world.

So where is this social world? Fortunately, it can become more visible to us with a little playful comparison. Imagine that someone has taken an old bedsheet to a public place, doused it in gasoline in the presence of a crowd, and put a match to it, inciting those gathered to stomp their feet, shout, and gnash their teeth in anger. The picture seems odd, doesn't it? We might wonder why people were so upset. Now imagine that the old bedsheet is a national flag. You can see why the crowd would react in anger. In both cases we had someone burning a rectangular cloth. What was the difference? The social world invests a symbol (the flag) with meaning.

Symbols do not simply refer to either subjective interiority or objective things, but rather they evoke a social world, the shared reality among us. When someone says, "The blood of the martyrs is the seed of the church," we don't expect to see some ecclesiastical farmer (maybe Tertullian) tending a furrowed field waiting for clapboard buildings to emerge from the ground. We recognize instinctively that such language is designed to help us understand our shared reality as church, not to offer us objective directions for church growth. By the same token, if someone says, "The heavens are telling the glory of God," we don't ask the psalmist (Ps. 19:1) or even Franz Joseph Haydn to undergo psychiatric evaluation.[17] Such symbolic language is designed not so much to express inner subjectivity as to call forth a shared understanding of God's relation to creation.

INTERPRETING THE SOCIAL WORLD
IN FRONT OF THE TEXT

We begin with a clarification. Biblical scholars have long been interested in matters of social world. However, their interest traditionally has been in something different: the world behind the text. What we propose to consider is the social reality, the symbolic universe, rendered available in front of it. Paul Ricoeur offers an orientation to help us get at this kind of world: "what has to be appropriated is nothing other than *the power of disclosing a world* that constitutes the reference of the text" (emphasis mine).[18] In other words, we are looking at how such symbols function, how they disclose the world.

How do we get there? Peter Berger and Thomas Luckmann offer a model for understanding how social worlds and their symbols arise, maintain themselves, and change.[19] Social worlds begin when human beings engage in cooperative activity. In the process they develop the objects and symbols of common life, culture. In the course of that activity they generate a symbolic world that over time becomes self-evident enough to seem to stand apart from its producers (in the church we call this "We've never done it that way before"). In the last recurring stage, that symbolic world—

even though it is a human product—acts back to shape the minds of its producers. Thus the symbols of that humanly produced world acquire meaning by virtue of human activity, achieve a perceived givenness as a result of that activity, and then actually begin to shape and/or perpetuate the human consciousness that produced it.

For example, imagine with the help of Berger and Luckmann a society in its infancy—a few people gathering at a lagoon to fish for subsistence. Over time they realize that when working together they can get enough fish to feed the whole lot of them for a year. Cooperation, after a while, becomes increasingly stereotyped as the society develops and new generations come along. At first, certain repeated acts become routinized features of the society: how to sew a net, how to put together a canoe, how to dry fish—perhaps even certain rituals pertaining to the fishing season. Over time, as the founders die and more generations are born, this repeated activity begins to beget something of a worldview. Certain virtues are cultivated and vices punished, depending on what makes a good fisher (patience, solidarity with other fishers) or a bad one (noisy, a "rock skipper"). At later stages of this fishing society's development, the range of this social world is extended symbolically to the cosmos. Now, generations after its founding, when a member of this once "primitive" society looks heavenward, she tends to see constellations of stars that to her look like various kinds of fish (perhaps Pisces?) and "The Big Canoe" (whose tip points to the Fish-pole star), and she calls an arresting looking galaxy "The Great Lagoon." Even though her distant ancestors created this society, its symbolic universe now shapes her awareness and sense of meaning in the cosmos.

From the example we can see how Berger and Luckmann's model might help preachers wrestle with the very cosmological questions that apocalyptic texts pose. Symbols, though human creations, represent a society's way of ordering reality, a clearing amidst the disorder of chaos, for meaningful human activity. Pastors naturally become aware of this any time they deal with a symbol in parish life: the placement of the furniture in the chancel, the use of certain memorial gifts like candles on high church holidays, or perhaps even the location of the flag. Pastors new to a church likely know that such objects are sometimes symbols of profound order and life in the congregation. The same is true of apocalyptic symbols. They intend to offer a clearing of meaning in the midst of chaos.

What is more interesting for us, however, is the way in which social worlds go "cosmic." Over time, these symbols are the means by which human beings invest not just local spaces (like churches or chancel areas) but the *whole cosmos* with meaning.[20] It is this totalizing tendency of religious reflection, this "cosmization," which gives us a framework for under-standing the significance of the cosmic range of apocalyptic symbols. Why, after all, does Genesis call the sun and the moon the greater light and the lesser light? Some scholars argue that they are countering a Babylonian cosmology, for which the sun and the moon were gods. In other words, religious symbols are often not just matters of the individual heart; with great frequency they stream out into space to render the whole universe meaningful.

Given the interesting relationship between human beings and their social world, we also have at least three ways in which symbols can function. At the beginning of our lagoon example, we saw how reflection on human activity gave birth to new symbols. At this level symbols have an important role to play in "world construction." Later as the social world is perceived as inscribed in the heavens, symbols participate in the task of "world maintenance." That is, symbols help to legitimate a social world and to promote or sanction certain kinds of meaningful activity. Even then, one other moment is also possible in the life of social worlds. At points where chaos overwhelms order, there is the possibility of "world delegitimation."[21]

A social-world approach to symbols holds much potential for interpreting New Testament apocalyptic texts. Instead of assuming the fixity of worldviews (such as an ancient, mythological worldview and the modern, scientific one) and struggling mightily to bridge the two-thousand-year gap, our analysis can assume a variety of approaches to social worlds. If nothing else, the sociologist's description of symbolic worlds should yield for us at least three ways of relating to them symbolically: world construction, world maintenance, and world delegitimation.

Of course, all this talk about "stances toward world" seems foreign to our experience. Yet how we relate to social worlds symbolically also shows up in how we do our pulpit ministry.

Symbols and World Construction

Symbols can be used to help construct social worlds. Do you remember the impact of Martin Luther King Jr.'s "I have a dream" speech in Washington, D.C., in 1963?[22] With his innovative use of some of the most powerful foundational myths and symbols in the dominant culture of the United States, King succeeded in reshaping the racist landscape of the country into an inviting vision. Of course, his speech did not eliminate racism in North America. Racism still persists today. Yet his speech did succeed in changing profoundly the way in which North Americans looked at themselves and in empowering others to join with him in the struggle. Homiletician Richard Lischer writes:

> Through the breadth of his appeal to Western values and his creative use of the Judeo-Christian tradition, his rhetoric helped create a fragile and temporary consensus among people of good will in America. . . . Like no preacher in the twentieth century, King transposed the great Judeo-Christian themes of love, suffering, deliverance, and reconciliation from the sacred shelter of the pulpit into the arena of public policy and behavior.[23]

In a very real sense, King's dream offered a new world for us to inhabit.

Symbols and World Maintenance

For preachers the maintenance of a social world through symbols surfaces most clearly at funerals. When someone dies, chaos seems to disrupt a society's order. As pastors we know that we must do something to help maintain the social world under the threat of chaos. Within the parish, conversation seeks to maintain something of a meaningful world: "I guess the Lord just needed him up there in heaven." "It was just her time to go." Or, at the casket, "He looks so peaceful."[24] While such conversation may be more or less helpful theologically, it represents an attempt by the community at making meaning—to hold the chaos of death at bay. Yet the importance of ongoing "conversation" for world maintenance is also why we preachers instinctively feel that the funeral sermon is so important. We are keenly aware that our words, our core shared symbols, help not only the grieving individual in the pew, but also the community which must somehow integrate this chaotic breach in their common life.

Symbols and World Delegitimation

In many ways "world delegitimation" is the rarest of the three stances toward world for the preacher. Social worlds are not easily taken apart. Yet it does happen. Here the powers-that-be are shown to be sham powers. A skillful preacher may well focus on aspects of our awareness that we don't normally talk about and simply confess the truth that we've all suspected in our heart of hearts all along. It's like Paul saying to the Corinthians, "Deep down, we know that those powerful idols in the temples are truly nothing."[25] It's like the little girl in the fable saying, "I don't see any clothes—the emperor is naked!" It's like Dorothy no longer fearing the Wizard of Oz because she knows it is just a man behind the curtain. Here cosmic symbols of an old order are debunked.

Preaching on the Edge of the Abyss:
Apocalyptic Symbols and Negotiating Social Worlds

We saw in chapter 1 that the definition of the genre apocalypse deals with the important connection between apocalypses and negotiating symbolic worlds:

> Apocalypse is a genre of revelatory literature . . . intended to interpret present, earthly circumstances in light of the supernatural world and of the future, and to influence both the understanding and the behavior of the audience by means of divine authority.[26]

Perhaps a social-world approach to the symbols of New Testament apocalyptic texts allows preachers to consider more explicitly how such worlds relate to their own.

We have seen already that preaching is always engaged in negotiating worlds. Social worlds are inherently precarious things that require conversation to keep them going. Sometimes even a word can make them totter ("Loose lips sink ships!"). Preachers can legitimate a "social world" by exploring its symbols and affirming their value, as in our funeral example above. They can begin to construct a social world with radical acts of theological naming, as in Martin Luther King's "I have a dream" speech. Preachers can also shake a social world's foundation by bringing to speech ways in which a symbol no longer "holds" in their hearers' awareness, such as exploring interpretations of Jesus' death on the cross that are used in the perpetuation of abusive behavior toward others.[27] Given these different possibilities, preachers would do well to use symbols, apocalyptic or otherwise, with pastoral discernment. When we preach, we are doing more than expressing ourselves or offering alternative points of view. We are actually engaging in an activity that potentially shatters an old world or announces a new creation.

Given what we've learned about symbols and social worlds, the Kaffeeklatsch with Sigmund and Karl need not have been so frustrating. True, Freud and Marx got bogged down disputing whether the *campesino*'s Lukan crucifixion scene from *The Gospel in Art by the Peasants of Solentiname* was about intrapsychic struggles between the Ego and Superego or was simply an example of religion as the opiate of the people. Tellingly, Ernesto Cardenal includes a dialogue about the Lukan crucifixion in the page opposite the painting. These Nicaraguan Christians clearly grasp the power of symbolic change for becoming liberative agents in their social world:

"I tell you truly that today you'll be with me in Paradise."

ERNESTO: The man talked to him about his kingdom, and Jesus talks to him about Paradise. In Genesis Paradise had been presented as something that there was at the beginning of humanity. But the intention of the biblical writer was not to present us a past that we were to yearn for in vain (the Bible never looks backward) but to present to us a *utopia,* a future goal for humanity. The prophets speak of Paradise as something that would be in the future, and they identified it with the messianic era. And Christ says that Paradise (his kingdom) begins now, that afternoon. With his death. He died while all Jerusalem was celebrating Holy Week. So while he was dying on the Cross, in every house they were eating the ritual paschal lamb—just as David Tejada was beaten to death on Good Friday, at the hour when they were making the Stations of the Cross on the streets of Managua. And his body was then thrown into the crater of the Masaya volcano.

WILLIAM: The Christianity that we had was very false, and every year we heard about the Passion, but we didn't understand it the way we now understand what Good Friday is. *Now we're gradually understanding it and we're gradually having courage to stand up to things.* (emphasis mine)[28]

When we change the world symbolically, we open up the possibility for changing ourselves and the world around us. The symbols we use in preaching can disclose new possibilities for human action. In fact, sometimes some people actually call it *Word of God.*

FROM THE FIG TREE LEARN ITS LESSON: SOCIAL-WORLD READINGS OF APOCALYPTIC SYMBOLS

Now let us finally put our musings about apocalyptic symbols into practice. Most of the work is in fact fairly instinctive. The key is to avoid reducing the symbols to "referents" or "subjective feelings" and to try to understand the symbols as a negotiation of a social world. An easy way to begin this process is to use the four steps listed below.

Step 1: Identify the Symbolic Allusions in the Text

This kind of work requires both study and free association. A great place to start is with your own imagination. When you hear symbolic language about blood, what do you think of? Perhaps more importantly, what biblical uses of the symbol does it remind you of: covenants with patriarchs and matriarchs, systems of sacrifice, Christ on the cross, Lord's Supper? Once you've allowed yourself to play with the symbol, get down to work. Look again at an annotated Bible or, better, the *Greek New Testament*. In the margins you will frequently find concrete scriptural allusions that may well be informing the word choice here. If these are lacking, a good commentary can locate some for you.

Step 2: Look at How the Symbols Function in Other Texts

Now take the symbolic allusions you have gathered and see how these same symbols have been used elsewhere. Is the "day of the Lord" a day of judgment or salvation? Some of both? Then what is it for Israel and what is it for Israel's enemies? It is important to ask questions of perspective here since some of our own symbolic associations may be out of step with biblical symbols or the ways in which they are typically used.

Step 3: Compare and Contrast These Uses of the Symbol with Your Text's

Using the evidence from the other texts alluded to, make your best judgment as to how this symbol is being used in your text. Does the symbol announce the demise of an oppressive social world? Does it announce the overturning of your world of privilege? It could be both, you know. Does the symbol offer a vision of a new reality coming into view? Does it come on the scene as promise or threat? Does the symbol try to shore up the cosmic order against the onslaughts of chaos? These "stances toward the social world" embodied in the text's symbols are what you must determine.

Step 4: Consider How the Symbols Can Shape the Hermeneutical Stance of the Sermon

David Buttrick argues that introductions establish a hermeneutical orientation for the sermon.[29] With the information you now have about how the symbols function, try to figure out how you can shape the sermon to the kinds of meaning-making the symbol calls forth. This is especially important since a literalistic sermon introduction can sink you. In other words, if you raise the issue of the "literal truth" of these or any symbols, you'd better be ready to answer the questions that raises. Instead, let your reading of the symbols be not an object to talk about in your sermon but a hermeneutical lens for rereading the social world you live in.

A Test Case: A Social-World Reading
of Apocalyptic Symbols in Mark 13:24–37

We begin of course by noting the inescapably social nature of apocalyptic symbols in this text. The world into which apocalyptic symbols irrupt is a world of fixity, a world whose universe of meaning is projected into the heavens, the sacred canopy. By borrowing the language of the sociology of knowledge to describe the backdrop of Mark's apocalyptic symbols, we recognize that we are dealing with realities that are somewhat more than metaphorical, somewhat more than "history" in the strict sense. Yet we assert baldly that such apocalyptic symbols are profoundly real and historical in the sense that they are profoundly social. This presupposition will guide our reading.

Mark 13:24–27 contains the most apocalyptic fireworks. Therefore, this will be our primary focus. Here we have numerous allusions to Hebrew Bible texts which help us to locate Mark's symbols within a wider tradition.

> The sun will be darkened, and the moon will not give its light, and the stars will be falling from heaven, and the powers in the heavens will be shaken. (Mark 13:24b-25, my translation)

These opening verses might seem at first blush to be offering signs of an impending historical cosmic cataclysm. That is how we might well hear and interpret them—pure threat! Yet the many scripture allusions here point to a different understanding. Isaiah 13:10 reads: "For the stars of the heavens and their constellations will not give their light; the sun will be dark at its rising and the moon will not shed its light." Yet this is not a portent of judgment against creation, but is part of an oracle against Babylon! For Israel these are signs attending the day of the Lord, a socially configured "cosmic cataclysm" that precedes the divine advent. The social world of Babylon is being undone! So for Israel these are not signs of judgment, but of promise. Even the words about sun and moon have to do with the deconstructing of the Babylonian gods (read: powers-that-be). The same could be said for the many parallel texts from Joel (2:10; 3:4, 15). They have to do with the coming of God, the day of the Lord. To be sure, they were signs of judgment "for the nations"; not, however, for faithful Israel. Isaiah 34:4 picks up some of the same symbols: "All the host of heaven shall rot away, and the skies roll up like a scroll. All their host shall fall, as leaves fall from the vine, like leaves falling from the fig tree" (RSV). Here the host of heaven represents God's earthly enemies. Again, the object here is a deconstruction of the powers-that-be using the symbolism of cosmic cataclysm in the context of an oracle of judgment against God's enemies. In short, verses 24–25 use the apocalyptic symbols of advent not to awaken fear of some kind of cosmic cataclysm, but as a sign to awaken hope—a hope that powers in the heavens, those who sit on thrones and preside over the systems that seem to be fixed and eternal, are being shaken to make way for the day of the Lord—that great and terrible day!

> Then they will see Humanity's Child (the Son of Man) coming in the clouds with much power and glory. (Mark 13:26, my translation)

The clearest reference here is to Daniel 7:13: "I saw in the night visions, and behold, with the clouds of heaven there came one like a son of man, and he came to the Ancient of Days and was presented before him" (RSV). Interestingly, the son of man in Daniel arrives in the context of divine judgment (Dan. 7:9–14) in that he arrives after the slaying of the beasts. Yet none of that is present in verses 24–27. In Mark's text Humanity's Child arrives not on the heels of judgment, but just in time to gather the elect to salvation. Such a reworking of apocalyptic symbols is crucial for understanding our text. In both cases the arrival of Humanity's Child is done in the context of signs of theophany, for example, the clouds. Yet what is lacking in Mark's reworking of that theophanic symbol is its connection with judgment and punishment.

> Then he will send the angels and gather together his chosen ones from the four winds—from the edge of the earth to the edge of heaven. (Mark 13:27, my translation)

Here we hear echoes of Zechariah 2:6, where a mention of the winds is made in connection with the return of the exiles home. In addition we attend to the familiar sounds of Deuteronomy 30:4: "If your outcasts are in the uttermost parts of heaven, from there the Lord your God will gather you, and from there he will fetch you" (RSV). Essentially, our text combines the images from both to give a rather overwhelming picture of salvation—from the four winds, the edge of earth, *and* the edge of heaven. Yet this exercise in salvific hyperbole forces us to re-envision our entire apocalyptic symbol system. If the speech's setting on the Mount of Olives (see chap. 3), the "watch out" parenesis of 13:5b–23 (see chap. 2), the cosmic cataclysm of verses 24–25, and the arrival of Humanity's Child caused us to expect the bloodiest of judgments, hearers must surely find themselves surprised. Instead of judgment, hearers get a gracious picture of salvation entirely without the vivid beast slaying and consumption by fire that they would expect. Even the cosmic cataclysm of verses 24–25 is not seen as judgment, but as a necessary prelude to a salvific advent.

This is also demonstrated by the subsequent symbol of the fig tree. As we noted in chapter 3, the fig tree is first the object of curse in Mark 11. Yet now it is a figure of immanent salvation. Clearly the reworking of apocalyptic symbols is happening throughout the Markan narrative!

The use of the symbol of the fig tree—a figure from the cyclical world of nature—opens up yet another question relevant to our theological analysis of apocalyptic symbols here: namely, how we understand apocalyptic time. Yet perhaps this problem and the problem of our own encounter with the rhetoric of delay in the text (see chap. 2) cannot make sense within the horizon of historical imminence but only within the context of the radical *immanence* of the mythic imagination.[30] It is this sense of time that will continue to prevail in our own symbolic understanding. Prior to the figure of the Lord of the house, all of the language concerning time is indefinite: when (ὅταν). At the point where the hearers' understanding of watching is transformed from Βλέπετε to γρηγορεῖτε—the praxis of watching actively—only then is the language of definitive time used: "when" as a point in time (πότε). Our theological appropriation of this material then will necessarily be guided by a different sense of time, one which sees time from within a specific location. In a community that sees itself within the horizon of the eschatological sign of resurrection, the baptismal sign of new creation, and the eucharistic sign of proleptic banquet, such language of mythic immanence makes sense. Similarly, then and only then does the radical call to a new praxis of "watching" actively also make sense—only from within such praxis can we talk about imminence.

Symbolic World from Text to Sermon

The apocalyptic symbols we have unpacked seem to call forth ambivalence. On the surface we hear these symbols as terrible judgment. There is something simply terrifying about a "world" falling apart. Yet a closer look at how these symbols function from a social world perspective shows that these symbols have more to do with undoing an established world of the powers (esp. vv. 24–25) and then announcing a liberating salvific free-for-all (vv. 26–27), complete with exodus-like clouds of divine presence. This fundamental ambivalence of judgment and salvation should inform our sermon. It can do so in at least two ways.

First, it will be important to establish the sense of initial dread the symbols evoke. The best way to do this is to make our hearers aware of places where their "world" seems to be falling apart. Assuming the rhetorical destination (chap. 2) and the formal route (chap. 3) of the sermon have already been established, it will be important to establish this as a hermeneutical orientation: the focus will be on how we see "ourselves in the world" and not just the objective world as bare facticity. In other words, the sermon must begin at the level of *perception* and speak accordingly. We do not need someone telling us that these are end-time signs, but rather we need someone who can help bring to the surface for us how we already *perceive* ourselves in a precarious world.

Second, the liberative and salvific side of the apocalyptic symbols in Mark 13:24–27 should surface in connection with the realization noted earlier that this apocalyptic form parodies the typical theophany form. In other words, that reversal should help us "see" our shaky social world within the marvelous light of God's emerging salvation. Again, the point will not be simply to say: "Gee, isn't it obvious that the world's getting better?" Clearly it is not—and such Pollyanna talk will only provoke smirks and giggles. We need to bring out aspects of life as lived where we see salvation, God's odd liberation, acted out in our world's rubble.

---

1. *The Tennessean,* Thursday, Nov. 10, 1994, section A.
2. Phillip Scharper and Sally Scharper, eds., *The Gospel in Art by the Peasants of Solentiname* (Maryknoll, N.Y.: Orbis, 1984), 63.
3. Ach, du Lieber! By accident you seem to have invited a spokesman for "vulgar Marxism" to coffee. According to my seminary colleague and resident historian, Prof. Oscar Cole-Arnal, vulgar Marxism reflects an earlier, thoroughgoing materialist phase of Marx's thought rather than his later, presumably less vulgar, *dialectical* materialist period.
4. Elisabeth Schüssler Fiorenza, *Revelation: Vision of a Just World* (Minneapolis: Fortress, 1991), 7.
5. Ibid., 8–9.
6. Annotation to Dan. 7:4–8, in *The New Oxford Annotated Bible with the Apocrypha: An Ecumenical Study Bible* (New York: Oxford Univ. Press, 1991), 1138.
7. John Collins notes that turn-of-the-century historical-critical scholarship, represented by R. H. Charles, was wooden and rigid in its interpretation of apocalyptic texts (*The Apocalyptic Imagination,* 2d ed. [Grand Rapids: Eerdmans, 1998], 14–16).
8. W. Sibley Towner, *Daniel* (Atlanta: John Knox, 1984), 95.
9. N. Porteous, *Daniel: A Commentary* (Philadelphia: Westminster, 1965), 106–7.
10. On one level what we have here is the struggle between what New Testament scholar Norman Perrin called "tensive" and "steno" symbols. Tensive symbols are more opaque and allusive, while steno symbols tend to be more transparent, one-to-one statements. Curiously, in his earlier work, Perrin was fairly sure that apocalyptic symbols were on the "steno" side ("Eschatology and Hermeneutics," *Journal of Biblical Literature* 93 [1974]: 11). Later, Perrin shifts to say that at least some apocalyptic symbols may actually be "tensive" (*Jesus and the Language of the Kingdom* [Philadelphia: Fortress, 1976], 31).
11. Belshazzar's reign began in 548 B.C.E.; Antiochus Epiphanes' in 175 B.C.E.

12. Kurt Tucholsky, "Bilder aus dem Geschäftsleben," in *Gespräche, Diskussionen, Aufsätze*, ed. I. Feix and E. Schlant (New York: Holt, Rinehart & Winston, 1969), 51.

13. Paul Ricoeur in A. Lacocque, *The Book of Daniel*, trans. David Pellauer (Atlanta: John Knox, 1979), xxi–xxii.

14. Ibid., xxii.

15. This is where I part ways with the impressive work of Elisabeth Schüssler Fiorenza. In her commentary on Revelation, she argues that an appreciation of Revelation's allusiveness is the province of scholarly readings that prefer not to pin down their readings with historical moments and contexts (Fiorenza, *Revelation*, 18–20). Conversely, "typological" readings, which take the experience of oppression in history as grounding any proper hermeneutical move, are the province of the oppressed (ibid., 10–12). I am trying to propose another way of viewing the problem. Instead of embracing the text's allusiveness in the name of endlessly indeterminate readings, I wish to propose that an open-ended yet analogical reading invites us to reconsider our overly closed readings of our own context. Such a method, to my mind, takes these difficult texts with great seriousness while refusing to let a context of privilege close us off from the text's claims.

16. When someone is addressed in the New Testament, the koine Greek second person plural ὑμεῖς, its declensions, and its correlative verbal conjugations in the New Testament are far more common than its singular συ counterparts. By this writer's computer count, the four cases of the second person plural appear 1,840 times in the *Greek New Testament*. By contrast the four cases of the second person singular appear 1,069 times.

17. Franz Joseph Haydn, *The Creation Oratorio* (New York: C. F. Peters, 1795–98).

18. Paul Ricoeur, *Interpretation Theory: Discourse and the Surplus of Meaning* (Fort Worth: Texas Christian Univ. Press, 1976), 92.

19. Peter Berger and Thomas Luckmann, *The Social Construction of Reality* (New York: Doubleday, 1966). The notion receives an especially useful summary treatment in chap. 1 of Peter Berger's *The Sacred Canopy* (New York: Doubleday, 1969).

20. As a sociologist, Berger can talk about symbols as humanly constructed projections on the cosmos. Lurking beneath these technical issues are, however, profoundly theological and philosophical ones. If Berger is right, Feuerbach wins. Our symbols point not to God but to our projections of God. Nonetheless, I choose to use his sociological approach for three compelling reasons. First, Berger himself acknowledges that he does his work from the empirical frame of reference of the sociologist. This, even for him, does not preclude the possibility that "the projected meanings may have an ultimate status independent of man [*sic*]" (*Sacred Canopy*, 180). Second, his sociological perspective is clearly useful as an explanatory tool for the "social-world" symbols of apocalyptic texts. Third, even if his position is theologically and philosophically problematic for the kind of symbol analysis we are considering here, we have, since Origen, a long Christian tradition of "plundering the Egyptians," that is, freely using the resources of those who would hem us in while we are being led to a land of freedom and promise.

21. Berger discusses the idea both generally and in relation to the theological task in *Sacred Canopy*, 96, 179–85.

22. Martin Luther King Jr., "I Have a Dream," in *A Testament of Hope: The Essential Writings of Martin Luther King, Jr.*, ed. James M. Washington (San Francisco: Harper & Row, 1986), 36.

23. Richard Lischer, "Martin Luther King Jr.," in *Concise Encyclopedia of Preaching*, ed. W. Willimon and R. Lischer (Louisville, Ky.: Westminster John Knox, 1995), 290.

24. Berger and Luckmann underline the importance of such conversation for world maintenance (*Social Construction of Reality*, 152ff.).

25. See 1 Cor. 8:4.

26. Adela Yarbro Collins, "Early Christian Apocalypticism: Genre and Social Setting," *Semeia* 36 (1986): 2, 7.

27. Pamela Cooper-White, *The Cry of Tamar: Violence against Women and the Church's Response* (Minneapolis: Fortress, 1995), 94.

28. Scharper and Scharper, *The Gospel in Art*, 62.

29. David Buttrick, *Homiletic* (Philadelphia: Fortress, 1987), 90–91.

30. See chap. 2, n. 20.

Chapter 5

Preaching and the Maintenance of World: A Homiletical Exegesis of Revelation 5:1–14 (Easter 3C)

[5:1] Then I saw in the right hand of the One seated on the throne a scroll, written on the front side and back side and sealed with seven seals.

[2] Then I saw a strong angel proclaiming with a loud voice, "Who is worthy to open the scroll and loosen its seals?" [3] And no one in heaven or on earth or under the earth was able to open the scroll or to scan it. [4] And I cried much because no one worthy was found to open the scroll or scan it. [5] And one of the elders said to me, "Don't cry; look! The lion of the tribe of Judah, the root of David, has overcome to open the scroll and its seven seals.

[6] Then I saw between the throne and the four creatures and the twenty-four elders a Lamb standing, though slain, having seven horns and seven eyes, which are the seven spirits of God sent out to all the earth. [7] And he came and received it from the right hand of the One seated on the throne. [8] And when it received the scroll, the four creatures and the twenty-four elders fell down before the Lamb, each one having a harp and golden bowls filled with incense, which are the prayers of the saints. [9] And they sang a new song, saying,

"Worthy are you to take the scroll and to open its seals; for you were slain and with your blood redeemed for God people from every tribe and tongue and people and nation; [10] and made them for our God a kingdom and priests; and they shall reign on earth."

[11] Then I saw and heard the sound of many angels encircling the throne and the creatures and the elders. And their number was ten thousands of ten thousands and thousands of thousands, [12] saying with a loud voice,

"Worthy is the Lamb who was slain to receive power and wealth and wisdom and strength and honor and glory and praise."

[13] And I heard all creation in heaven and on earth and below the earth and on the sea, and everything in them saying,

"To the One seated on the throne and to the Lamb be praise and honor and glory and power for eons of eons."

[14] And the four creatures said, "Amen." And the elders fell down and worshiped.[1]

INTRODUCTION

Until now we have been dealing with a single text: an apocalyptic theophany seemingly smuggled into Mark's Gospel in chapter 13. By venturing into the heart of Revelation, however, it seems we have entered the Beast's lair. Here we have a full-blown, twenty-two-chapter Apocalypse. Applying our threefold approach to Revelation should be a real test of its usefulness.

Yet as we enter the odd world of the Apocalypse, it is also important to adjust our method to this very different text. We will still do rhetorical, generic, and symbolic analysis, just as we did with Mark 13. Yet the Apocalypse of John is decidedly different from the apocalyptic discourse in Mark in one very important way: John's Apocalypse is largely a "narrative," while Jesus' words in Mark 13 are a speech. As a result, we will rely a little less on rhetorical analysis (which focuses more on speeches and how they persuade) and a little more on genre analysis. Why? Although the apocalyptic theophany form represents only three verses of Mark 13:24–37, the form that we will study in Revelation 5 makes up the whole text.

It is curious that the New Revised Common Lectionary prescribes from Revelation 5 only a snippet (vv. 11–14) for the Third Sunday in Easter, Year C. As preachers of the gospel, however, we need not feel ourselves bound to overly atomized lections—even those offered by well-intentioned lectionary committees. Therefore, we will try to understand our Eastertide Revelation text within its wider context.

WHERE IN THE WORLD WE ARE GOING:
AN "EXPANDED CAST" AS HOMILETICAL DESTINATION

In order to find out what our sermon on Revelation 5 might do, we must first figure out what the text is doing. Once again, we must pay attention to the rhetorical effect of our text, that is, how it might impact hearers.

Fortunately, Revelation's narrative gives some indications that it was written to be read aloud (Rev. 1:3; 22:18). Therefore, we will use rhetorical criticism here looking in the narrative for oral and written markers that cue us in on what this text is trying to *do* relative to hearers.

Step 1: Determine the Rhetorical Unit

Without discerning the text's rhetorical boundaries, it will be hard to figure out where the text is "coming from" and where it is "heading." Looking closely at the narrative, it is clear that Revelation 5 is only the second half of a two-chapter scene set in the heavenly throne room.[2] With Revelation 5 an important shift takes place. Revelation 4 mostly gives a detailed description of the heavenly throne room. Revelation 5, by contrast, is marked by a return to plotted action. The plot is now governed not by lavish description, but by a narrative *complication:* Who is worthy to open the scroll in the right hand of the One seated on the throne? It is the working out of this question that drives the action in the throne room.

Yet Revelation 5 also supplies *oral* markers that set off this section. Unlike Revelation 4, which seamlessly presents vivid details in a unified picture, Revelation 5 asks its hearers to look first at one thing, then the next. How? Through the use of a repeated phrase, "Then I saw" or "Then I looked" (Rev. 5:1, 2, 6, 11). By means of these oral markers, the seer focuses our attention not on a single panoramic scene, but on a series of dramatic actions.

With these narrative and oral boundary cues for our rhetorical subunit, we can begin to discern what Revelation 5 is trying to do. The action begins at the throne (5:1). Yet with every one of the seer's "Then I saw/looked" statements, the circle of characters around the throne widens. First, the action focuses solely on the One seated on the throne, who holds the seven-sealed scroll (5:1). With the next "I saw" (5:2–5) the action now shifts to a strong angel, the weeping seer, and a comforting elder. With the third "I saw" (5:6–10) the action spirals out to include even more characters: the Lamb standing though slain, the four living creatures, and the twenty-four elders, who acclaim the Lamb "worthy" (5:8–10). The final "I saw" (5:11–14) then draws the circle of characters even wider to include not only living creatures and elders, but many angels and every creature in heaven and on earth and under the earth and in the sea, and all that is in them—all of whom sing an acclamation to the Lamb and the One seated on the throne.

The narrative movement and oral markers thus begin to cue us in on what this text is doing: namely, *expanding the cast* of those participating in and impacted by the text. The passage starts in the heavenly equivalent of the oval office in the solitary presence of the "One seated on the throne," but it does not end there. By the end of our rhetorical subunit in Revelation 5, all creation is involved in doxological action. The rhetorical movement of the text spirals out from the throne to include the whole cosmos (see figure 3).

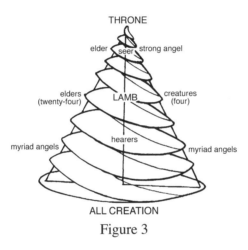

Figure 3

Step 2: Analyze the Rhetorical Arrangement of the Text

Since Revelation 5 is a narrative, and not a speech, we can devote ourselves simply to a close reading of the four parts that make it up. In this way we will find out what is specifically at stake in "expanding the cast."

Section 1 (Rev. 5:1) is short and to the point. It sets the scene by starting at the throne and describing the mysterious seven-sealed scroll. The gravity of the scene sets the tone for the hearers: the scroll, in the very right hand of the One seated on the throne, is important.

Section 2 (Rev. 5:2–5) then proceeds to draw hearers into a wrenching complication. An angel asks: "Who is worthy to open the scroll and break its seals?" As if listening to the events through the seer's ears (the point of view in the narrative is the seer's), we learn that no one in heaven or earth is found worthy. When the seer cries that no one was found, thus using the *pathos* of the moment to carry hearers along, one of the elders comforts him by saying: "Don't cry; look! The lion of the tribe of Judah, the root of David, has overcome to open the scroll and its seven seals."

This, however, makes the dramatic action in section 3 (Rev. 5:6–10) all the more startling. Two features here are worth noting.

First, the figure who shows up looks very little like a "lion" or Davidic royalty: it's "a Lamb standing, though slain." This opens up a potential gap for the hearers. Either the elder was wrong in section 2 (given the importance of the elders in our text, this is unlikely), or something about this Lamb *redefines* the messiahship connoted by the terms "lion of the tribe of Judah" and "root of David" (Rev. 5:5). By placing the two sets of images so closely together, hearers are invited to consider messianic vindication in light of suffering. Yet because the symbol is a "Lamb," it may be that the seer's language is designed to evoke another surprising connection. This "Lamb" may well be a symbol of *Passover*. Just as the slaughter of the Passover lamb is remembered as the beginning of the liberation from Egypt, so also this Lamb marks the start of an opening to freedom. In that case, the surprise is even greater: the Lamb standing though slain, the crucified and risen one, is also the Lamb who betokens a coming liberation— an exodus into freedom.

Second, once the mysterious Lamb receives the scroll, the focus of the dramatic action moves immediately downward:

the Lamb takes the scroll

↓

the heavenly court acclaims him "worthy"

↓

their song draws implications for us below

↓

What implications? "For you were slain and with your blood redeemed for God people from every tribe and tongue and people and nation; *and made them for our God a kingdom and priests; and they shall reign on earth.*" In Revelation 5:10 the Passover allusions become even clearer.[3] Rhetorically, celebrating the Lamb's Passover act of making a royal, priestly people suddenly puts the hearers in a new position: *within the throne-room liturgy.* As the worthy song is played out—a heavenly occurrence—we hearers below overhear from the very throne room what this celestial drama means for us. In other words, the song's mention of people "redeemed for God . . . from every tribe and tongue and people and nation" (5:9–10) suddenly puts *those* who overhear in the action. Hearers who listen in on the living creatures and elders' song learn of their destiny indirectly: "a kingdom and priests [who] shall reign on earth."

Section 4 (5:11–14) then continues the dramatic flow by expanding the celestial cast to include even more. The "worthy" song of the angels, living creatures, elders, and myriads reworks the earlier "Who is worthy?" question (5:2), now including both God *and* the Lamb. Then section 4 outdoes even itself by featuring all creation's praise: a kind of cosmos-wide salvific finale. With an ending like that, what more can you do? The seer punctuates it with the worship of the elders and an "amen" from the four living creatures.

The text's cosmic praise functions for hearers as a lavish doxology. The acclamations are positively effusive. Why the elaborate praise scene? Some argue Caesar was surrounded by his own hyperbolic liturgy and attended by fawning hosts wherever he went. Some link Revelation's acclamations to a usurping of the imperial liturgy of Rome.[4] Perhaps Revelation 5 is John's *christological* reinterpretation of the imperial establishment's massive claims for Caesar. For though the empire's power consists in dealing death decisively to its enemies, the Lamb standing though slain would seem in his very person to loosen its deadly grip. And that might be something worth singing about.

Step 3: Analyze the Text's Arguments and Style

After our close reading of the arrangement of the rhetoric in Revelation 5:1–14, there is little to say about its arguments and style. From a rhetorical standpoint, most of what a narrative text uses to develop its argument actually belongs to its literary form, which we will cover below. Suffice it to say, when dealing with a narrative text rather than a speech, the rhetorical features of an apocalyptic text tend to recede while the literary and generic elements become more prominent.

At any rate, we have now seen what this text is trying to do. John's vision seems to want to "expand the cast" of celestial characters from the throne outward to all creation. The move is not just cosmetic. The downward action from heaven to earth begins at the throne, passes through the Lamb standing though slain, includes an announcement of the hearers' coming status as exodus-like royalty and priests, and then evokes the praise of the whole cosmos. In short, Revelation 5 intends in and through the reality of suffering a dramatic "expanding of the cast" for the purpose of liberation.

HOW IN THE WORLD WE ARE GETTING THERE: CHRISTOLOGICAL INVERSION FROM LION TO LAMB

Our rhetorical analysis has given us a destination: expanding the cast for liberation. Now we turn to analysis of the generic form that underlies the text. The key apocalyptic form for understanding our text seems to be the "throne-room vision." In Revelation 4—5, the form looks like this:

seer describes throne (4:2–3)

+

seer describes heavenly court (4:4–5:3)

+

seer cries: no one worthy to open seals (5:4)

+

elder assures seer (5:5)

+

Lamb gets/takes commission to open seals (5:6ff.)

Although a form like this throne-room vision may be new to us, its precursors can be found in prophetic literature and subsequently linked to other apocalyptic texts.[5] We can use this analysis of the form in our search for earlier texts.

Step 1: Identify Antecedents for the Form in the Hebrew Bible

First Kings 22:19–23, Isaiah 6, Ezekiel 1—3, and Ezekiel 10 are the Hebrew Bible antecedents for the throne-room vision form. These texts use "throne scenes" to signal impending judgment on *God's people and/or their representatives.*[6]

Just as the knock-knock joke usually uses five constant elements, so the form of these throne texts uses three.[7] The column on the left shows the three formal elements, while the text from 1 Kings in the right column shows how the form typically works.

A. Throne Described
B. Court Described

I saw the LORD sitting on his throne, with all the host of heaven standing beside him

E. Commission

to the right and to the left of him. And the LORD said, "Who will entice Ahab, so that he may go up and fall at Ramoth-gilead?" Then one said one thing, and another said another, until a spirit came forward and stood before the LORD, saying, "I will entice him." "How?" the LORD asked him. He replied, "I will go out and be a lying spirit in the mouth of all his prophets." Then the LORD said, "You are to entice him, and you shall succeed; go out and do it." (1 Kings 22:19b–22)

Step 2: Look for the Form in Jewish Apocalypses

Although we found three formal elements in some similar Hebrew Bible texts, in apocalypses we discover the form has added two more. Here we see the full-blown form known as the "throne-room vision."[8] Overall, we can find eight throne-room visions in seven different apocalypses which we can plausibly date prior to or roughly contemporaneous with Revelation (4—5): *1 Enoch* 14:18–16:3 (*Watchers*); *Testament of Levi* (3:4–8; 4:2–6 and 5:1–2); Daniel 7:9–18; *1 Enoch* 90:20–22 (*Dream Visions*); 60:1b–10 (*Similitudes*); 71:5–16 (*Similitudes*); *2 Enoch* 20–22 (shorter recension); and *Apocalypse of Abraham* 18–20:5.[9]

As with their Hebrew Bible cousins, virtually all the throne-room visions in apocalypses begin with the throne, move to the heavenly court, and end with the commission (*and/or* an announcement). What is new in apocalypses is this: between the description of the heavenly court (**B**) and the commission (**E**) are *two new elements*. The first is a report of fear, typically the visionary's (**C**). The second is an attempt to assure the fearful seer (**D**).[10] The column on the left below lists the typical parts of the apocalyptic throne-room vision form. Excerpts from *1 Enoch* 14:18–16:3, in the column on the right, may give a feel for the shape of the form in Jewish apocalypses:[11]

A. Throne Described

[. . .] And I observed and saw inside it [the second of two heavenly houses] a lofty throne—[. . . .] And the Great Glory was sitting upon it—as for his gown, which was shining more brightly than the sun, it was whiter

B. Court Described

than any snow. None of the angels was able to come in and see the face of the Excellent and the Glorious One; and no one of the flesh can see him—the flaming fire was round about him, and a great fire stood before him. No one could come near unto him from among those that surrounded the tens of millions (that stood) before him. He needed no council, but the most holy ones who are near to him neither go far away at night nor move away from him. Until then I was

C. Seer's Fear

prostrate on my face covered and trembling. And the Lord called me with his own mouth

D. Assurance

and said to me, "Come near to me, Enoch, and to my holy Word." And he lifted me up and brought me near to the gate, but I (continued) to look down with my face. But he raised me up and said to me with his voice, "Enoch." I (then) heard, "Do not fear, Enoch, righteous man, scribe of righteousness; come near to

E. Commission

me and hear my voice. And

> tell [. . .] the Watchers on
> whose behalf you have been
> sent to intercede—[. . . .] Tell
> them, 'therefore, you will have
> no peace.'[12] (*1 Enoch* 14:18a;
> 14:20–15:2a; 16:3c)

Of course, apocalyptic throne-room visions do more than add new formal elements. The commission (**E**) changes in throne-room visions in apocalypses. In the Hebrew Bible, a prophet or a heavenly figure was commissioned to speak a word of judgment to the prophet's people or king. In apocalyptic throne-room visions, however, the commissions usually involve an announcement of a change in the seer's status. In other words, the commission both announces judgment on opponents and, in all but two cases (*1 Enoch* 14—16 and Daniel 7), singles out the seer for some sort of elevation of status.[13]

Apocalypses use the throne-room vision form in yet another unique way. We noted earlier that the Hebrew Bible antecedent texts used throne-room visions to sanction announcements of judgment against prophet's own people or their king. In apocalypses the throne-room vision typically comes before a cosmic tour or a vision of judgment and/or salvation. In every case, however, any judgment associated with the visions is not for the seer's community but for their enemies: the unrighteous, the beasts, and so on. Apocalyptic seers, therefore, tend to use the throne-room vision to justify still other visions that subsequently offer mysteries of the cosmos (*1 Enoch* 14:18–16:3 > 17ff.), hope for the righteous (for example, *1 Enoch* 71:5–16 > 71:17), and/or vindication against their enemies (such as Daniel 7:9–10 > 7:11).

Step 3: Compare the Form with Your Text

We have now established a baseline for reading Revelation 5:1–14 as part of a throne-room vision. Typically this apocalyptic form includes five elements:

A: description of throne
B: description of heavenly court
C: expression of seer's fear
D: assurance/explanation of event to seer
E: commission/announcement of seer's new status

The form typically precedes other visions — usually cosmic tours or visions of judgment and/or salvation. The throne-room visions typically legitimize the seer as a recipient of the visions and mysteries that follow.

In some ways, Revelation uses the apocalyptic throne-room vision form in expected ways. Just as a "Knock, knock" evokes a "Who's there?" in Revelation 5 the expectation of the typically apocalyptic throne-room vision plot is met. The judgment in Revelation's seal and bowl cycles comes with the understanding that God has the people's *salvation* in mind.

Yet Revelation's use of the throne-room vision also thwarts some of the expectations that its form would evoke. While in all the above texts the throne and the heavenly court are never confused, in John's throne-room vision a novel character appears among the *dramatis personae* of the heavenly court, the Lamb standing though slain, who actually approaches the throne! This movement from the court to the throne, from relative immanence to transcendence is unheard of in throne-room visions.

This remarkable addition to the form is also confirmed by the formal movement of the text. Whereas the apocalyptic throne-room vision typically moves through the **A-B-C-D-E** formal sequence, Revelation's throne-room vision changes the order by shifting the seer's role to the Lamb in elements **C** to **E**. How? In Revelation 5:1–14 the seer does not express fear (**C**) so much as grief because no one is worthy to open the seals. Then the seer is assured (**D**), not so as to assume a commission (**E**), but to be comforted with the *Lamb's* fulfillment of the commission to open the seals and the *Lamb's* "elevation in status." Apocalypses typically use throne-room visions to authorize seers and their visions. Revelation 5 seems to take a different tack. Its focus is less on the seer than on Christology. Instead of having the seer's exaltation in view, this throne-room vision exalts the Lamb "standing, though slain." You might envision it this way:

> Knock, knock!
> Who's there?
> Seer.
> Seer who?
> Not seer-who, *who's-here:* the Lamb!

Step 4: Determine the Significance of Your Text's Use of the Form

Our look at the throne-room vision form in the Apocalypse, its Hebrew Bible precursors, and its parallels in other apocalypses has given us a useful baseline for interpreting our lection. In many ways Revelation 5 meets the expectations that its form evokes. However, the ways in which it has varied the form are startling.

Above all, John's use of the throne-room vision form invites us to follow the route of a christological inversion of expectations. Most throne-room visions invite readers and hearers to believe the fantastic visions that follow them because (*a*) they come from the heavenly throne room, and (*b*) an authoritative and elevated seer says so. Revelation 5, however, offers a different route. Here the focus is not on the seer. In fact in our text, the focus shifts decisively to the Lamb for its authorization. This is important for two reasons that both surprise and confirm hearers' expectations.

First, it is surprising because the Lamb symbol, introduced into the narrative here and not earlier, at the very least transforms messianic expectations. The slain Lamb stands in metaphoric tension with both the elder's assurance (the lion and the Davidic root) and the formal expectation of an elevated seer in the heavenly throne room. So the use of the form forces us as hearers to reevaluate our messianic expectations.

At the same time, the image is also confirming of hearers' expectations. It is precisely the Lamb who was slain who "stands" in the heavenly throne room between creatures and elders and who ultimately takes the scroll from the right hand of the One seated on the throne. Regardless of whether the communities John addressed experienced real persecution or only perceived it (a matter of some scholarly dispute), the image confirms something important: one who suffered "with us" or perhaps "like us" has been vindicated. Indeed, his solidarity in suffering with us is the key to unraveling what is to come. The Lamb standing though slain is alone worthy to unseal the scroll.

Form of Text and Form of Sermon:
The Route of Christological Inversion

Our study of the throne-room vision form in Revelation 4—5 has now yielded a route for our sermons: christological inversion. Whereas the form initially causes us to pin our hopes on elevated seers, outwardly and unambiguously strong messianic pretenders (lions and Davidic roots), the ambiguity of the "Lamb standing, though slain" gives us something to preach. Thus, as we consider how to arrive at our homiletic destination, "expanding the cast toward liberation," it will mean taking a route that is unexpected: a messianic path not marked by the success stories of the powerful, but a christological path that links liberation and suffering, exodus and the cross.

The question for the preacher is then this: Where do we tend to imagine messiahs as ultimate projections of human strengths? Who are our human demigods and how do they skew our perception of Christ crucified and risen, like a Lamb standing though slain? More importantly, where is it that we recognize that suffering and liberation are joined in our experience? A sermon on this text that wishes to move toward its rhetorical destination will need to do so with care. It will require a christological route, one that passes through the cross.

HOW SIGNS WILL SHOW US THE WAY: REVELATION 5's SYMBOLS AND MAINTAINING AN ALTERNATIVE WORLD

We have seen how the text's rhetoric intends to expand the cast. This in-clusion of a greater number of characters in the throne-room liturgy has un-derscored the move from the throne to all creation by means of the Lamb. The Lamb, after all, is the one who inaugurates a Passover-like redemption for those who "overhear" and for the whole cosmos. We have also seen how the seer used a common apocalyptic form in order to play on hearers' expectations. Although grounding his work in the typical features of the throne-room vision, he shifts his hearers' focus from the seer to the Lamb. In the process, the people of the audience hear themselves paschally re-named as eschatological priests and kings.

Between rhetorical intention and generic expectation, however, some-thing more is going on in Revelation 5. Indeed, the very fact that the scene begins in heaven and by the end ranges over the whole cosmos testifies to that. Thus, in order to understand better what is at stake in these cosmic, apocalyptic symbols, we turn to a symbolic analysis of the text.

Our first reaction to visionary material like the symbols of Revelation 5 is the best place to start. In short, the picture strikes us as fantastic, literally "out of this world." In this way, Revelation 5 is quite unlike Mark 13, whose apocalyptic symbols intrude into our everday world for a scant three verses (13:24–27) before returning to the normal reality of fig trees and house-holders (13:28–37). Revelation for the most part remains in the heavens, in the throne room, and shows creation *joining* the heavenly praise chorus.

As such, the symbolic language represented by a throne, four living creatures, twenty-four crowned elders, a seven-horned and seven-eyed Lamb standing though slain, and myriad angels will function differently. In other words, the concern here goes far beyond the content of the sym-bols. For this reason steps 1 and 2 from the previous chapter are superfluous here. Thrones, living creatures, and angels are just run-of-the-mill throne-room characters. In this case, what is most interesting about these symbols is their function together as a world. How is it that such a fantastically different world affects this everyday world that we know—the one represented by embracing a loved one, paying property tax assessment bills, and punching the time clock at work? In other words, what happens when symbolic worlds collide?

Let us assume that the symbolic world in front of the text (the fantastic world of Revelation 5) and our world are meant to be mutually interpretive. This is to say that this "other" world offered by Revelation 5—a symbolic world filled with a throne, living creatures, elders, the Lamb, and myriad angels—wishes to speak with ours for a moment.

To do so requires, however, a suspension of both disbelief and belief. The disbelief refers to whether or not we can be open to such a fantastic world. Sure, on the surface, it seems hard. The seer's world is, after all, weird. Yet we actually suspend such disbelief all the time: when we allow the fantasy of science fiction to help us imagine the future in a new way, or better, when we allow the depth image of a symbol (say, a broken loaf) to call us, at least for a moment, out of our success anxieties to revel in the incalculable absurdities of grace. Indeed, we actually do this every time we pray the Lord's Prayer in the Eucharist. There we pray it with our own lips: "Thy kingdom come, thy will be done, on *earth* as it is in *heaven.*"

We are ultimately a people of divided minds. Because we are social creatures, we live in more than one symbolic world at a time. The question is how to negotiate them.

Of course, as good Christian people, we must avoid one mistake. This creation we share is not up for negotiation. Creation itself has its own bare facticity. We cannot dream it away, we cannot will it away. But then again, why should we? God called it good.

But perhaps our *symbolic* worlds are not meant to be quite so closed, so impervious to change. Unlike creation, they are humanly constructed (see chap. 4). Could it be that from time to time worlds become so closed that they need to be toppled for humanity to flourish? Perhaps so.

The symbols of Revelation 5 are bringing something important to light. When a world does seem closed (say, a world under the heel of empire), perhaps it is good to remember that other symbolic worlds may be drawing us forward into more habitable places to live. It is as true as ever that Rome, or Moscow, or Washington, D.C., cannot be wished away. We can close our eyes all we want, but when we open them they will still be there. Nonetheless, whenever we worship and offer praise to God, we are acknowledging another Presence whose being is *not* dependent on the triumph of the world we take for granted—even if our presence seems to be. And that Presence, we remember, both suffered and died in a world like ours and was raised as the firstborn of *new* creation. That Presence who knows our flesh and our suffering intends something much more for us than 401k's (RRSP's in Canada), hermetically sealed suburban homes, and lives numbed by the flicker of the cathode ray tube. This Presence intends freedom, communion, and the fulfillment of creation.

This, then, brings us to the second part. If we must suspend disbelief, we must also suspend belief in the inevitability of the social world we inhabit. In other words, we need to be open to the fact that our symbolic world of everyday life is also constructed. While it feels fixed and we assume it has always been there, it has not. Think, for example, how many times we have heard about "the global economy" over the past few years. If we watch the nightly news, we get a dose of it every evening! Now, though, think back to when you first heard the term. It probably wasn't that long ago. So why do we live as if the global economy "ever was, is, and shall be, world without end"? Perhaps because social worlds' symbols are compelling enough to make us think they are. In order to hear the alternative world of Revelation 5, however, we need to be invited to suspend not only disbelief but belief—in a world that seems closed, but in the long run is not.

This means that something of great social magnitude is at stake in the symbols of Revelation 5. The seer's rhetoric offers hearers an apocalyptic, exodus-like symbolization of themselves as liberated from an old world ("redeemed for God people from every tribe and tongue and people and nation") for a new one ("and made them for our God a kingdom and priests; and they shall reign on earth"). Although the comfortable, middle-class part of us would like to ignore it, the impact of such symbols cannot be spiritualized away. These apocalyptic symbols of exodus are, after all, fundamentally political and economic ones.[14]

Nonetheless, we have also seen how John both presupposes and yet *changes* the mythic throne-room vision narrative. In doing so, the seer is also engaged in a profound symbolic transformation. At the center of the vision is not just a lion or even a powerful seer, but the Lamb. And if this Lamb is slain yet standing, then the hope that John allows his audience to overhear in 5:10 is plausible. Moreover, as the slain Lamb actually approaches the throne in heaven and is hymned by all creation, so John's hearers can engage in resistance to an old world, knowing that the Lamb has "made them for our God a kingdom and priests; and they shall reign on earth." As such, John deploys the apocalyptic scene so as to offer a vision, a "symbolic universe," capable of evoking not just a different image of themselves, but a different social world and a different way of engaging the old one.

Symbolic World from Text to Sermon

We have argued that an understanding of symbolic language actually offers a hermeneutical orientation for preachers. This is no less true with Revelation 5.

Clearly preachers would be laughed at, and rightly so, if we turned the visionary material into a heavenly tour. The symbols are not interested in mediating information so much as they are intended to alter perception.

The challenge for preachers is therefore twofold. First, how can we help hearers imagine the claims that dual symbolic worlds make? We can begin by sensing those places where we feel them in our bones. Are the people in the pews of God's "new creation" or are they religious consumers? Are we who pastor ministers of Word and sacrament or ecclesial CEOs in albs and stoles? These sample questions help us focus on how we concretely live out in our lives the claims of colliding worlds. Second, we can reflect on how various artistic endeavors function. What is it about plays, movies, or the visual arts that offer alternative perceptions to our own? Do they draw our taken-for-granted world of everyday life into question? Do they begin to draw us out of what we assume into some other life-giving possibility? Of course, preachers should be careful. Sometimes art exists to keep the lid on things, too. This means preachers may want to think carefully about how their worlds work symbolically on them and how symbols, whether in art or elsewhere, try to act back on us.

In the end, however, preachers will need to be careful not to overpromise. Apocalyptic symbols may be misused if they become just another entertainment or palliative from the world's pain. We have argued that John the seer is using these symbols in order to encourage a praxis of resistance among his hearers. Perhaps a proper focus for us is not to consider how we can use symbols to imagine the world away or to imagine a new one into being. Rather, our goal is more modest: to begin, even if in just small ways, to imagine ourselves in the world *free by the grace of God.*

FROM EXEGESIS TO SERMON

So what do we preach this Eastertide? First, we set as our destination a "widening of the cast" to include even our hearers as "a kingdom and priests." Second, we preach more than the lectionary prescribes. The cosmic doxology of 5:11–14 can turn demonically triumphalistic without the ironic subversion of the throne-room vision's form in the slain Lamb's appearance. So let us mimic that subversion homiletically by considering our own cultural messianic longings and then the mystery of Christ crucified: the Lamb standing, though slain. Third, the symbolic world of the text invites us to think of ways of "maintaining" or perpetuating the alternative reality that is John's vision. As a result, we will try to find places of tension where worlds collide and discern ways in which we can confirm the life the gospel offers us in the world. Theologically, the danger will be to hold those two realities absolutely apart. Our theology of creation should be our guide here. God so loves the world . . . still. Rather, what we will do is to hold those two worlds together and trust that God can use them for transformation in the here and now.

Given our destination, our route, and the signs along the way, the sermon's structure might proceed thus:

> To us human beings the future is a mystery.
> So what do we want? A messiah who can wrangle out a happy ending.
> But look at God's choice for messiah: the Lamb Jesus!
> Of course, this Lamb is actually a sign of God's Passover for us.
> So now we are free for God's royal future for us.

Since the scene proceeds dramatically (the "worthy songs" sound like operatic recitatives!), we could frame the whole sermon within a dramatic image as a way of establishing the claims of competing symbolic worlds. This way we also free our hearers from wooden literalism for the metaphoric power of John's vision in Revelation 5.

---

1. Once again, this translation is mine. Some of the wording I use will seem odd, until one realizes that the words chosen in English are designed to *do* something rhetorically and are orally analogous to the Greek. In Greek, some of the key words of the text sound alike, for example "seals" and "slain" (σφραγῖδας/ ἐσφάγης, brought together in 5:9), "scroll" and "scan" (βιβλίον/βλέπειν, brought together in 5:3). My translation is an attempt to bring these aural associations, however awkwardly, into the English translation. Those who have a further interest in how "sound clusters" like these may affect the meaning of a text may want to chase down the work of Bernard Brandon Scott and Margaret Dean ("A Sound Map of Mark 7:1–23," paper delivered at the SBL Annual Meeting in Chicago, Nov. 22, 1994).

2. The wider context of our text is relatively easy to confirm rhetorically. On either side of Revelation 4—5 are markers that indicate a shift of time, place, and characters. Chapters 1—3 deal with John's initial vision while on the island of Patmos. In the context of his vision, the Son of Man commands John to write the seven letters, which make up the bulk of Revelation 2—3. In Revelation 4, however, all this changes. An indication of time change comes right at the beginning: "After this," the seer writes (4:1). As for the shift in place, John is now invited through an open door in heaven (4:1). As for characters, before John now are a whole new cast: a throne with One seated on it (4:2), twenty-four elders in white robes (4:4), and four "living creatures" (4:6).

   Similar changes mark a shift out of our throne-room scene at the conclusion of Revelation 5. The focus has moved from the characters in the throne room and those who are praising and acclaiming God to a white horse and its rider (6:2). Why? A new action has begun with the loosing of the first of the seven seals. With each seal yet another new character is introduced along with a new set of dismal, earthly consequences (6:3–17). Given the change in content from effusive hosts in heaven and on earth to a Death-ridden pale-green horse (6:8), we can safely conclude that we have moved from one rhetorical unit to the next.

3. In Ex. 19:6 the title is used in connection with a liberation remembrance at the foot of Mount Sinai.

4. Elisabeth Schüssler Fiorenza, *Revelation: Vision of a Just World* (Minneapolis: Fortress, 1991).

5. Christopher Rowland, *The Open Heaven* (New York: Crossroad, 1982).

6. In 1 Kings, Ahab, Israel's king, receives Micaiah's doom oracle conveyed from the heavenly throne room. Similarly, Isaiah is called to prophesy destruction to his own people after seeing God on the throne with an attending host. In Ezekiel the prophet also receives a commission to preach after having seen the throne.

7. The question of what constitutes the throne-room vision form is a matter of some scholarly dispute. The chief issue seems to be in determining the form's relationship to another form: the call narrative. While I am convinced that the form of the throne-room vision, though historically related to the call narrative form, is distinct, readers may wish to consult other perspectives on the issue. Some commentators see the form as relatively simple and limited mostly to the texts we propose (David Heinrich Muller, *Ezechiel-Studien* [Berlin: Reuther & Reichard, 1895], 8–10; Claus Westermann, *The Praise of God in the Psalms* [Richmond: John Knox, 1965], 99–100; and Walther Zimmerli, *Ezekiel 1* [Philadelphia: Fortress, 1979], 97–100). Two other scholars argue that the throne-room vision is not a distinct form apart from other call narratives, but part of a tradition that includes the calls of Moses and Gideon. Norman Habel develops an elaborate six-part description of the form ("The Form and Significance of the Call Narratives," *Zeitschrift für die alttestamentliche Wissenschaft* 77 [1965]: 297–323). Later, Benjamin Hubbard traces his sevenfold form from Hebrew Bible texts through other literature and all the way to Matt. 28:16–20 (*The Matthean Redaction of a Primitive Apostolic Commissioning* [Missoula, Mont.: SBL/Scholars, 1974], 62–64).

8. Several scholars have attempted to treat the question of the form in apocalyptic literature. Matthew Black follows part of Zimmerli's conclusions, yet links his form decisively to apocalyptic texts in Daniel and *1 Enoch* ("The Throne-Theophany Prophetic Commission and the 'Son of Man': A Study in Tradition

History," in *Jews, Greeks, and Christians: Essays in Honor of W. D. Davies,* ed. Robert Hamerton-Kelly and Robin Scroggs [Leiden: Brill, 1976], 57–73). However, Black is more interested in tracing the development of the Son of Man motif using tradition-history than in the formal shape of these texts. Other scholars tracing some of the relationships between our Hebrew Bible antecedents and apocalyptic texts are Christopher Rowland ("Visions of God in Apocalyptic Literature," *Journal for the Study of Judaism in the Persian, Hellenistic, and Roman Periods* 10 [1979]: 138–54) and Ithamar Gruenwald (*Apocalyptic and Merkavah Mysticism* [Leiden: Brill, 1980]). Judging by his conclusions, however, Rowland ("Visions," 152–54) seems more interested in the visionary's experience and the revelation of spatial mysteries than in truly literary concerns. Both here and elsewhere (*The Open Heaven* [New York: Crossroad, 1982]) Rowland moves more or less thematically and historically through the texts with little literary interest. Gruenwald, to his credit, attempts to set up a literary template for his reading of apocalyptic and *merkavah* texts (*Apocalyptic,* 31). Yet his own evidence lacks the breadth of support across texts to justify setting it up as representing the vision's "characteristic features." Perhaps the best work to date on tracing the literary form into apocalypses is John J. Collins's *Daniel; with an Introduction to Apocalyptic Literature* (Grand Rapids: Eerdmans, 1984), 18. Collins sees the form consisting in two essential elements (throne and attendants) and two "typical" (*Daniel,* 119) motifs (fire and angelic singing).

9.   For the problems of dating associated with these texts, see n. 17 in chap. 3. In addition to the apocalypses cited, we find three incomplete versions of throne-room visions in "related types" which could also be plausibly dated before 100 C.E.: 4Q S1 40 24 2–8; 4Q403 1 ii 1–16; and 4Q405 20 ii 21–22. John Strugnell, who first published his translation of 4Q S1 40 24 2–8, dates the text on paleographical evidence to 75–50 B.C.E. ("The Angelic Liturgy at Qumran," in *Congress Volume,* VTSup, vol. 7 [Leiden: Brill, 1960], 336, 343). The other two texts come from the Sabbath *Shirot* first published and translated by Carol Newsom in *Songs of the Sabbath Sacrifice: A Critical Edition* (Atlanta: Scholars, 1985). Newsom dates our final two texts, 4Q403 1 ii 1–16 and 4Q405 20 ii 21–22, paleographically along with the others to "the late Hasmonean and early Herodian periods" (*Songs,* 1). In addition to these, however, one other nonapocalyptic text from this period also gives evidence of the form: *Ezekiel the Tragedian* 68—82, which R. Robertson dates to the second century B.C.E. ("Ezekiel the Tragedian," in *The Old Testament Pseudepigrapha,* ed. James Charlesworth [New York: Doubleday, 1983], 2:804). But since this text is neither an apocalypse nor a "related type," it will not come under the purview of this investigation. Indeed, since we operate in Revelation 4—5 with a throne-room vision form *in* an apocalypse, for purposes of comparison we will give pride of place to the eight throne-room visions in the apocalypses cited above.

10.   Element **C**, the seer's fear, appears in *1 Enoch* 14:24a, 25b; *Testament of Levi* (3:9 only, not in 5:1–2 proper); Daniel 7:15; *1 Enoch* 60:3; 71:11; and *2 Enoch* 20:1c (and repeated through the formal cycle twice in 21:2c, 4a, and 22:4!). With regard to the *Testament of Levi* text, we should note that elements **C**, **D**, and **B** do not appear in *Testament of Levi* 5:1–2, which is the throne-room vision proper. They do appear, however, in the immediately prior portions of the heavenly journey which the angel narrates for Levi's benefit (*Testament of Levi* 3:4–4:6). As the culmination of the narrated journey through the heavens, the an-

gel describes to Levi **A** the "Great Glory" dwelling in the uppermost heaven in 3:4 and **B** the worship of the archangels in 3:5–6. The element of fear **C** in 3:9 appears in the judgment theophany embedded within the heavenly journey (3:9–4:1). Words of assurance **D** and commission **E** are then given in the angel's second announcement in 4:2–6 (cf. 2:10–12). In a sense, the angel's narrated heavenly journey serves to preview the actual first person throne-room vision in 5:1–2, which contains only elements **A** and **E**! The upshot is that this brief throne-room vision proper in 5:1–2 serves to ratify the description, fear, assurance, and commission that the angel narrated earlier. This peculiar movement is, no doubt, in part due to the compositional structure and history of *Testament of Levi* 2—7. Marinus de Jonge carefully outlines the shape of *Testament of Levi*'s rather tortured narrative ("Notes on Testament of Levi II–VII," in *Studies on the Testaments of the Twelve Patriarchs* [Leiden: Brill, 1975], 258–60). Nonetheless, even with this compositional variation, the degree to which the angel's anticipatory narration conforms to the shape of our apocalyptic throne-room vision form is striking.

As for the *1 Enoch* 71 text, the fear motif is much clearer in Matthew Black's translation (Matthew Black, *The Book of Enoch or 1 Enoch* [Leiden: Brill, 1985], 68, 251) than in E. Isaac's (*Old Testament Pseudepigrapha,* ed. James Charlesworth [New York: Doubleday, 1983], 1.50). Black's reading and rationale for it appear in his commentary (*Enoch,* 68, 251).

Element **D**, assurance, appears in *1 Enoch* 14:24b–15:1, *Testament of Levi* (4:2 only, again, not in 5:1–2 proper; see preceding note); Dan. 7:17–18; *1 Enoch* 60:4–9; 71:14; and *2 Enoch* 20:2 (and repeated, as above, through the formal cycle twice in 21:3, 5 and 22:5–6a!).

Overall, these two new elements appear in 75 percent of our attested apocalyptic throne-room visions. Three-quarters of the throne-room visions in apocalypses begin with a pairing of elements **A** and **B**, thus establishing a typical movement of the form. When one adds in the narrative preview of the form in *Testament of Levi* 3—4 and the threefold cycle from *2 Enoch* 20—22, the pattern is ultimately attested in 82 percent of our literary exemplars. Elements **C** and **D** are likewise consistently attested in the apocalyptic throne-room vision form. Indeed, the motifs of visionary fear and assurance or explanation from a heavenly figure appear in 75 percent of our apocalypses overall. Furthermore, when **C** does appear in our texts, element **D** always follows. Together, these patterns for the deployment of our new elements provide more than sufficient warrant for viewing **C** and **D** as typical of the form. Finally, element **E** also appears in our apocalyptic throne-room visions with great consistency. Only one of the apocalyptic exemplars (Daniel 7) lacks it. In summary, our texts demonstrate rather clearly the typicality and durability of this form and its constituent elements across apocalypses. To be sure, the elements **C** and **D** are not entirely new. Elements of fear and assurance appear already in Isaiah 6 and Ezekiel 1—3 among Hebrew Bible throne texts. The difference with apocalypses is that the elements **C** and **D** appear with much greater frequency.

11. In a brilliant study on the motif of angel veneration, Loren Stuckenbruck argues that some of our texts represent other forms. Thus, for Stuckenbruck, incomplete variations on an "angelic refusal tradition" appear in *2 Enoch* 20, 21, and 22, of which the first two he designates an angelophany and the third a theophany (*Angel Veneration and Christology* [Tübingen: Mohr, 1995], 279–80). While it may

be that an angelophany introduces the rather extended and repetitious throne-room vision in *2 Enoch* 20—22, the presence of throne-room vision formal elements would still need to be accounted for.

12. E. Isaac, trans., "1 (Ethiopic Apocalypse of) Enoch," in *The Old Testament Pseudepigrapha,* ed. James Charlesworth (New York: Doubleday, 1983), 1:21–22.

13. Thus Levi becomes the "son," the blessing of the priesthood "until I (the Holy Most High) shall come"; Enoch, a heavenly scribe, Son of Man, or "like one of the glorious ones"; and Abraham, the father of many nations. Only two of our apocalypses do not seem to envision any kind of change of status for the seer: Enoch in the *Book of the Watchers* and Daniel.

14. Elisabeth Schüssler Fiorenza makes a compelling argument for such a perspective on Rev. 5:10 ("Redemption as Liberation," in *The Book of Revelation: Justice and Judgment* [Philadelphia: Fortress, 1985], 68–81, esp. 73–76). Latin American exegetes like Carlos Mesters (*El Apocalipsis: La Esperanza de un Pueblo que Lucha* [Medellín: Centro Ecumenico Diego de Medellín], 36) and Ricardo Foulkes (from an English precis of his *El Apocalipsis de San Juan: Un comentario desde América Latina,* Nueva Creación [Grand Rapids: Eerdmans, 1989], 1) have also pointed out this basic connection. Although not making the connection explicit, Allan Boesak's typological reading of Revelation 5:9–10 through the South African situation of *apartheid* exemplifies it nonetheless (*Comfort and Protest: Reflections on the Apocalypse of John of Patmos* [Philadelphia: Westminster, 1987], 60–62).

Chapter 6

Preaching and World Construction:
A Homiletical Exegesis of Romans 8:18–30
(Pentecost B)

[8:18] For I think that the suffering of the present time is not worth comparing to the coming glory to be revealed to us. [19] For the deep desire of creation awaits the revelation of the sons and daughters of God. [20] For creation was subjected to futility, not willingly, but on account of the one doing the subjecting, in the hope [21] that even creation itself shall be freed from the slavery of decay for the freedom of glory of the children of God. [22] For we know that the whole creation groans together and suffers labor pains together until now—[23] and not it alone, but even we ourselves, who possess the first fruits of the Spirit, even we groan among ourselves awaiting adoption, the redemption of our body. [24] For we were saved in hope; but hope seen is not hope, for who hopes for what one sees? [25] But if we hope for what we do not see, we await (it) with perseverance. [26] Likewise the Spirit also helps with our weakness. For we do not know how to pray as we ought, but the selfsame Spirit intercedes for us in inexpressible groans. [27] But the One who searches (people's) hearts knows what the Spirit's mind is, because it pleads for the saints according to God('s will). [28] We know that all things cooperate for good for those who are called according to (God's) plan. [29] Because those whom he foreknew, he also predestined to be conformed to the image of his son, so he would be the firstborn among many brothers and sisters. [30] And those whom he predestined, he also called. And those whom he called, he also justified. And those whom he justified, he also glorified.[1]

INTRODUCTION

This Pauline text affords great opportunities for preaching an apocalyptic word on Pentecost Sunday. Romans 8 is, after all, chock-full of references to the Spirit (esp. vv. 23, 26, 27).

Nonetheless, preachers must be wary of this text on two counts. First, the lectionary prescribes a textual unit that is less than helpful. Second, the groaning of believers here has often been romanticized to mean a kind of inward, wordless speech, a prayer that is somehow spiritually superior. By ranging beyond the narrow confines of the Revised Common Lectionary's textual boundaries, we can see that such "groaning" or "sighing" is not the product of a saccharine pietism, but a radically earthy manifestation of the apocalyptic turning of the ages. In other words, an apocalyptic motif lurks in this familiar Pauline text, a motif that may help us rethink what our sermon can *do* on Pentecost Sunday. Moreover, because of the unique way the apocalyptic symbol functions to rename the world, we may speak of the Spirit in a way that allows us to "preach in the new creation."

WHERE IN THE WORLD WE ARE GOING:
FROM SUFFERING TO GLORY GROANING
WITH THE SPIRIT AS HOMILETICAL DESTINATION

With Romans, of course, the use of our threefold method shifts slightly again. Because our text is not a narrative, the rhetorical analysis will be more important than it was for Revelation 5.

Step 1: Determine the Rhetorical Unit

Even an initial rhetorical analysis can help to clear up some misconceptions. The rhetorical boundaries of the text are clearly marked by the repetition of the word "glory" (δοξ-) at 8:18, 30. These indicate, respectively, the beginning and end of our rhetorical unit. Their positioning here and at a key transition point in our text (8:21) give us a first hunch. Paul wishes to say something about glory. If the opening at 8:18 is any indication, Paul is interested specifically in the connection between *suffering* and the glory that is to be revealed (ἀποκαλυφθῆναι). Likewise, if the last verses help us further discern what this text is doing, this same glory comes at the *end* of a divinely wrought process: "those whom he predestined, he also called. And those whom he called, he also justified. And those whom he justified, he also glorified." Paul's rhetoric may well intend to deal with glory, but neither without suffering nor without God somehow taking the lead.

Step 2: Analyze the Rhetorical Arrangement of the Text

Fortunately, the rhetorical arrangement or order of arguments can flesh out the reason why Paul is concerned with suffering and glory. A careful analysis of the rhetoric of the text yields the following structure:

> Introduction (v. 18)
> Topics (vv. 18–28)
>   A. The creation groans (vv. 18–22a)
>   B. Believers groan (vv. 22–25)
>   C. The Spirit groans (vv. 26–27)
>   D. Summary statement: "*all things* work together" (v. 28)
> Conclusion (vv. 29–30)

Note how Paul's topics start with what his hearers or readers already "know": all creation and believers "groan." Yet by placing the "Spirit" as the third in the series, he saves his best argument for last. This way, the groaning of creation and believers is "reinterpreted" as of the Spirit. At any rate, the relationship of the three topics (A, B, and C) and the summary statement (D) certainly precludes the notion that the Spirit's groaning is somehow "spiritual" from the top down! After all, the rhetorical arrangement demands that the groaning of creation, believers, and the Spirit be allied from the bottom up, not separated out as a romantic spiritualism would require. At the very end, the arrangement moves toward a "climax" in verses 29–30, which caps off the "bottom up" movement.[2] The "climax," the name of a rhetorical figure, refers to words arranged like a κλῖμαξ, a Greek term for ladder or stairs. What the rhetoric does at the end looks something like figure 4, which is to be read from bottom left to top right.

he also glorified.

↑

[30c] . . . those whom he justified,

↑

he also justified.

↑

[30b] . . . those whom he called,

↑

he also called.

↑

[30a] those whom he predestined . . .

↑

he also predestined

↑

[29a] those whom he foreknew,

Figure 4

One notices at the top of the stairs our rhetorical keyword: "glorified." The arrangement confirms our sense that this text intends something about glory—but above all, glory from the bottom up, a glory that *does*.

Given the bottom-up movement of the arrangement, the groaning language that dominates topics A–C is not in reference to an ecstatic spiritual escapism that eschews "words" and all creation with it. It is rather an expression of a radical solidarity of the church with the world, both of whom cry out to God for final redemption.[3] However, in the middle of groaning creation (8:18–22a) and believers (8:22–25) there is a surprise: the Spirit is present *there,* the same Spirit who is acting as their intercessor before God!

The arrangement has, therefore, filled out a critical piece of our homiletical destination. While the text's boundaries point us toward the juxtaposition of suffering and glory, the rhetorical arrangement tells us why. The groaning of creation and believers (Topics A and B) would seem to contradict any relation of suffering and glory (this worldly groaning and suffering are bad, while the glory to be revealed is good). For Paul, Topic C becomes his opportunity to rename the relationship of a groan-filled suffering and the glory to come as the work of the Holy Spirit. Such groans are more than a human response to one-damn-thing-after-another. Rather, with the Spirit they are birth pangs of something new. They are where we encounter our "being saved in hope"; they are where we find the Spirit "helping in our weakness."

Suddenly, our homiletical destination looks startlingly important: how is it that the Spirit's presence renames our suffering from the pain that has always marked human life in creation to the pain that comes with new birth?

Step 3: Analyze the Text's Arguments and Style

The notion of locating the Spirit in the groaning of creation and believers is unusual. Yet this radically social and cosmic understanding of groaning is reinforced by the language itself, that is, in terms of style. In Greek Paul has added the prefix "συν" ("with" or "together") to the main verbs of topic A in order to emphasize that all creation groans in travail *together*. Likewise we, the subject of topic B, groan "ἐν ἑαυτοῖς," *among* ourselves (not "inwardly," as some translations have it—the reflexive pronoun is in the plural!).

Now what the text *does* is becoming clear. Paul wishes to link suffering and glory because this is where the Spirit meets us. The arrangement doesn't offer an otherworldly spirituality from the top down, but evokes the presence of the Spirit precisely where new creation is being born—whether in creation or in believers. In other words, when we and creation are groaning, there is the Spirit: where the apocalyptic ages turn.

Beyond style, it is important also to consider the kinds of arguments used in a speech. Traditionally, speakers use three types of arguments: those that appeal to reason (*logos*), to the character of the speaker (*ethos*), and to feeling (*pathos*). We have seen that the rhetoric of the text grounds groaning in the context of suffering and glory. In verse 18 suffering is real enough, but it cannot be compared to the coming glory. While Paul uses some careful reasoning in his speech, the pathos-laden words of verses 19–28 serve an especially important function for him. The pathos, or appeal to feeling, reinforces for his hearers the placement of the Spirit in the rhetoric of suffering. Consider for a moment some of the words Paul uses here: "deep desire of creation," "subjected to futility, not willingly," "slavery of decay," "groans together," "suffers labor pains together," "perseverance," "weakness," "pleads," and so on. Tellingly, however, when we finally reach our glorious destiny in the final verb of verse 30 (ἐδόξασεν), we will have first been lifted up by not pure feeling, but theology!—the Pauline "climax" of God's plan, call, justification, and then glorification. Consequently, the rhetorical force of the Spirit here does not remain just a nice feeling, a tingle of the spine, or some holy comforter like an electric blanket. No, the Spirit "comforts" us by interceding for us before the throne and by standing in radical solidarity with us and all creation as we endure the futile final assaults of the old order (cf. 8:35–39) and understand ourselves again in the theological frame of those who are called, justified, and in the end, glorified.

Thus contrary to the typical ecclesial self-congratulation of Pentecost (such as, the "church's birthday"), Paul's rhetoric offers the Spirit as the down payment of glory *in order to help us to hope while we persevere in the suffering of the here and now*. This will be our homiletical "destination," too.

HOW IN THE WORLD WE WILL GET THERE:
AN APOCALYPTIC *ROUTE AND SIGN*
WITH THE WOMAN IN TRAVAIL FROM PAIN TO BIRTH

A rhetorical analysis alone, however, does not aid us in understanding what the relationship of groaning to creation, ourselves, and the Spirit fully means. For this we need to unpack the apocalyptic motifs and symbols that permeate Romans 8:18–30.[4] What we need to do is understand why it is so important for Paul to link the Spirit, "groaning," and "birth pangs" to the "revelation" of the children of God and the coming glory (notice the "apocalyptic" look to the Greek form of the verb "to be revealed" in v. 18, ἀποκαλυφθῆναι).

Note that we are shifting our usual tack with this generic analysis. Our rhetorical analysis gave no evidence that Paul is using in Romans 8 any sort of apocalyptic form at all. Instead, what we have are traces of apocalyptic motifs: things and people to be revealed, groaning, the Spirit, and birth pangs. So what do we do? We adjust our approach. While we will consider the Hebrew Bible and pseudepigraphal forms in which our apocalyptic motif appears, what formal evidence we have will actually send us immediately to analysis of the symbol: in this case, the motif of the "woman in travail."

It is important to note first off that the cosmic groaning of this text is not just generic. Literature both contemporaneous to and after Jewish apocalypses draws on the figure of the woman in travail as a stock element in the messianic woes (Mark 13:8; Matt. 24:8; 1 Thess. 5:3; and Rev. 12:2, for example).[5] Indeed, as New Testament scholar Dale Allison has noted, the Greek word ὠδίν (birth pangs) itself is something of a technical term for the messianic woes as early as the first century C.E.[6]

Step 1: Identify Formal Antecedents
for the Motif in the Hebrew Bible

The figure of the "woman in travail" is quite common in the Hebrew Bible. She shows up in historical books (Gen. 3:16; Ex. 15:14; 1 Sam. 4:19; and

2 Kings 19:3 [par Isa. 37:3]) and even in wisdom literature (Job 39:1–3; Ps. 48:6; and Lamentations 1). However, the figure is most prominent in prophetic literature, and in the various forms of prophetic speech like announcements of judgment, judgment oracles, salvation oracles, hymns, and so on (Isa. 13:8; 21:3; 26:17–18; 42:14; 66:7; Jer. 4:31; 6:24; 13:21; 22:23; 30:6; 48:41; 49:22; 49:24; 50:43; Hos. 13:13; and Micah 4:9). Almost all of the texts draw on the figure of the woman in travail to express the imminence and inevitability of a coming judgment. Virtually all of the oracles that use the figure sound something like this proclamation of judgment against Babylon:

> Pangs and agony will seize them;
>> they will be in anguish like a woman in labor,
> They will look aghast at one another;
>> their faces will be aflame.
>
> (Isa. 13:8)

Virtually every time the Hebrew Bible talks about the woman in travail, it is used as a means of expressing divine judgment.[7]

Step 2: Look for Formal Uses
of the Figure in Jewish Apocalypses

When we try to link the motif of the woman in travail to a formal history in Jewish apocalypses, we get bogged down. Why? The figure is used in only two Jewish apocalypses that could be plausibly be dated earlier than 100 C.E.: *1 Enoch* 62:4 and *4 Ezra* 4:40–42.[8] The latter text gives us a useful point of comparison with our Hebrew Bible texts:

> He answered me and said, "Go and ask a woman who is with child if, when her nine months have been completed, her womb can keep the child within her any longer?"
> "No, my lord," I said, "it cannot."
> He said to me, "In Hades the chambers of the souls are like the womb. For just as a woman in travail makes haste to escape the pangs of birth, so also do these places hasten to give back those things that were committed to them from the beginning." (*4 Ezra* 4:40–42)[9]

Yet with so few examples of the figure in apocalypses that are earlier than or about as old as Paul's letter to the Romans, a question remains. Why should we consider the woman in travail to be an apocalyptic figure in Romans 8:18–30?

For one thing, we must consider the use of the figure within the genre apocalypse. Wolfgang Harnisch has noted that while the woman in travail tends to be associated with announcements of judgment in prophetic literature, in apocalyptic literature it appears typically in announcements of salvation.[10] If Harnisch's tradition-critical study is right, Paul's use of this figure of the woman in travail is probably also an apocalyptic one. It is oriented toward not so much the pain of judgment as the birth pangs of God's new creation. In this way the use of the figure certainly parallels its use in apocalypses generally.

Second, there is something unique to his use of the image. Unlike the writers of other prophetic and apocalyptic texts cited above, Paul has stretched the use of the apocalyptic figure of the woman in travail by applying it not just to one entity (such as creation, Zion, the people, or even God as in prophetic and apocalyptic sources) but to all: creation, we ourselves, and the Spirit. Thus Paul embraces the apocalyptic use of the figure as salvific, while extending the embrace to include the entire cosmos!

Here, we will notice that our study of the *generic* use of the figure begins to shade off into a *symbolic* analysis of Paul's language.[11] In this way the symbol functions to rename the cosmos as a locus of the Spirit's action.

As such, what we have in Romans 8:18–30 is an apocalyptic figure used in world construction: we, creation, and the Spirit are symbolized as longing for new creation, "the freedom of the glory of the children of God," a glory that is to be revealed (ἀποκλυφθῆναι, v. 18). Symbolically, Paul is "cosmizing" the woman in travail figure to include all.[12] In other words, she has become a symbol by which to reinterpret the present reality. If groaning means for us a kind of wordless chaos and suffering, Paul wishes to reinterpret the groaning as the Spirit's creative work through the figure of the woman in travail. We don't groan for escape from the world, with the Spirit we groan for the crowning of God's new creation.

With this we finally encounter the third possible stance toward the "social world" that apocalyptic symbols offer. Mark 13 gave us an interpretation of the world as "falling apart," that is, Jesus' speech symbolically "delegitimizing" a world. Revelation 5, by contrast, was interested in enhancing the plausibility of an alternative world. In that case, the seer was symbolically engaged in an act of world maintenance. Here, however, we begin to see a third option. With Romans 8 we are invited into the cosmic delivery room to share in the birth of a new reality in the Spirit. The suffering of this present reality is actually heading somewhere. The pain experienced, the groans expressed, are birth pangs, signs of new creation.

FROM TEXT TO SERMON

A Theological Structure

So where does that leave us? We must preach about the Spirit this Pentecost Sunday, but we do not do so alone. For the groans of the Spirit are not just an expression of private spirituality but a sign of the new creation that is even now emerging.

The rhetoric has given us a destination: a Spirit-grounded perseverance in suffering toward a new world. Here the Spirit is discerned in a "cosmic" groaning from the bottom up that deepens our relationship to God's new creation. As we move toward this destination, preachers will want to ask: Where is the Spirit not "comfortable," but comforting in the etymological sense of the word (com = together; forte = strength)? Where are we strengthened together in the Spirit?

The genre analysis has given us a route. Whereas the groaning of the woman in travail is typically viewed as suffering in judgment in this world (especially in prophetic literature), in apocalypses the figure begins to cut a new way: as a sign of birth for the new thing God is doing. This reversal of the meaning of the figure of "groaning" in the Spirit will be an important part of how the gospel meets us in this apocalyptic motif. Are there places where we see our suffering not just as "one-damn-thing-after-another," but as a sign of new birth that goes beyond the individual to include the world God loves so much?

Our analysis of the figure as a symbolization of our world leads us to orient ourselves to an emerging new creation. The groans are not just ours, nor even the Spirit's solely, they are the groans of the cosmos, which has a stake in the new thing God is revealing (ἀποκάλυψιν, v. 19) through us. From a preaching standpoint, the hermeneutical question then arises: Where does God offer a vision of "new creation" by groaning through us and the cosmos even now?

Given what we've found about what in the world the text is doing, how it does it, and the signs we are given along the way, we can imagine a theological structure for our sermon that might help us do something similar.

> We Christians live in the Spirit.
> Yet we also live in a world groaning for release.
> Maybe that's why *we* groan for redemption, too.
> But we don't sigh alone—the Spirit sighs with us.
> That means the Spirit comforts us *through* pain to new creation.

CONCLUSION

So there we are. Our apocalyptic preaching with the Spirit need not be yet another narcissistic exercise in repainting the walls of human inwardness. Rather, our preaching of the Spirit is itself good news—good news for us and the whole creation!

---

1. Again, the translation is mine, and it is done a little awkwardly to highlight word and word root repetitions. These are frequently useful for rhetorical analysis and getting an oral sense of what the text *does*. For the value of such an approach, see chap. 5, n. 1.
2. For more information on this rhetorical figure, see George A. Kennedy, *New Testament Interpretation through Rhetorical Criticism* (Chapel Hill: Univ. of North Carolina Press, 1984), 28.
3. Ernst Käsemann, "The Cry for Liberty in the Worship of the Church," in *Perspectives on Paul* (Philadelphia: Fortress, 1971), 136.
4. Notice here I have combined steps 2 and 3. Since the apocalyptic material here is confined mostly to a single motif, our study of its use in the genre apocalypse and its function as a symbol can proceed together.
5. The notion of travail or birth pangs is also used figuratively outside of the apocalyptic scenarios above: namely, John 16:21 and Gal. 4:19, 27.
6. Dale Allison, *The End of the Ages Has Come* (Philadelphia: Fortress, 1985), 6 n. 6; see also 72–73. Allison's argument is in response to a claim by J. Christiaan Beker that the messianic woes doctrine can be documented only a century later in Jewish literature (*Paul the Apostle* [Philadelphia: Fortress, 1980], 146).
7. The important exception is Isa. 66:7.
8. Some might also be inclined to include *6 Ezra* 2:38–39 in this short list (Jörg Baumgarten, *Paulus und die Apokalyptik* [Neukirchen-Vluyn: Neukirchener Verlag, 1975], 175). For reasons of date and genre, however, it is probably best excluded from our list.
9. B. M. Metzger, trans., "The Fourth Book of Ezra," in *The Old Testament Pseudepigrapha: Apocalyptic Literature and Testaments,* ed. James Charlesworth (New York: Doubleday, 1983), 1.531.
10. Wolfgang Harnisch, *Eschatologische Existenz* (Göttingen: Vandenhoeck & Ruprecht, 1973), 68–69. However, given the evidence in the two texts we have identified from *1 Enoch*'s *Similitudes* and *4 Ezra*, it might be more accurate to say that apocalypses tend to include elements of judgment and salvation together.
11. Hence, the mixed heading at the beginning of this section! The methods exist for the sake of understanding, not understanding for the sake of the methods.
12. The term is from Peter Berger's work on symbols and their relationship to "nomos," *The Sacred Canopy* (New York: Doubleday, 1969), 20–51.

Chapter 7

Seeing Beyond: Developing an Eye for the Road

We have been traveling through a strange apocalyptic world together. We have been using three methods of approaching apocalyptic texts as a road map through that world. However, no one travels just for the sake of learning maps. Maps, even the best road maps, exist to enhance the joy of travel.

In the process of learning how to read such a road map, however, we can develop something useful: an eye for the road. When I first moved to Canada from the United States three years ago, I had to adjust to a different way of getting around. In Ontario, they don't call the major freeways "interstates," they call them "expressways." And if you're ever in doubt whether you are on an expressway or a four-lane highway, you obviously don't look for a red, white, and blue interstate shield. Instead, you check to see if the sign is green rather than white, or whether the number on the sign is one, two, or three digits. Three digits on a green background means expressway (such as the 401), one to two digits on a white background means a provincial or regional highway. At first I was always straining on the road, trying to read every sign to determine whether I was on the right one. Now after three years, I can tell even from a distance. I have developed an eye for the road in my new home.

The goal with apocalyptic texts is the same. Being clear about methods of biblical interpretation is not an end in itself. Rather, it is a means to an end: developing an eye for apocalyptic texts. Looking for what a text is *doing* does not mean slavishly following the three steps outlined in chapter 2 in perpetuity. Over time it means adopting a critical eye capable of seeing, even from a distance, what is coming down the pike. Similarly, doing genre analysis is not about tedious, methodical repetition. Instead, it is about developing an eye for how apocalyptic forms look. If it works, you may find yourself seeing apocalyptic theophanies in more texts than just Mark 13 (Matthew 24, Luke 21, 1 Thessalonians 4). No wonder the scriptures frequently describe the joy of finding! With a well-developed eye, you will discover that joy even in the parts of the Bible you may have been inclined hitherto to avoid.

AN EYE EXAM FOR DRIVERS:
THREE SAMPLE TEXTS FOR THE ROAD

As we consider three more apocalyptic lectionary texts, we will have a chance to try out whether we have developed eyes for the road. Each section will start with a scripture text. See what you notice as each text comes up.

Spotting an Apocalyptic Form for Our Homiletical Route:
1 Thessalonians 4:13–5:11 (Propers 27 and 28, Season after
Pentecost A)

[4:13] But we do not want you to be ignorant, brothers and sisters, concerning those who fall asleep, so that you be not bereft like the rest, who do not have hope. [14] For if we believe that Jesus died and rose, in the same way God will bring those who fell asleep through Jesus with him.

[15] For this we say to you by the word of the Lord: that we who are living, the ones left behind until the arrival of the Lord, shall not by any means come before those who fell asleep; [16] that the Lord himself, with a command, the archangel's voice, and God's trumpet, shall come down from heaven; and the dead in Christ shall rise first; [17] then we who are living, the ones left behind, shall be carried off with clouds to meet the Lord in the air; and thus we shall always be with the Lord. [18] Therefore encourage one another with these words.

[5:1] But as for the times and the seasons, brothers and sisters, you have no need of anything in writing. [2] For you yourselves know well that the day of the Lord comes like a thief in the night. [3] Just when people are saying "peace and security," then suddenly disaster comes upon them, like the birth pangs of a pregnant woman, and they shall not by any means escape. [4] But you, brothers and sisters, are not in darkness, so that the day should surprise you like a thief. [5] For you are all children of the light and children of the day. We are not of the night or darkness.

[6] So therefore, let us not sleep like the rest, but be wide-eyed and sober-headed. [7] For those who sleep, sleep at night; and those who get drunk, drink at night. [8] But let us, who are of the day, be sober-headed, wearing the breastplate of faith and love and for a helmet the hope of salvation. [9] After all, God did not destine us for wrath, but for attaining salvation through our Lord, Jesus Christ, [10] who died for our sake so that whether awake or asleep we together might live with him. [11] So encourage each other and build each other up one to another, just as you are doing.[1]

Did you catch the apocalyptic form embedded in Paul's letter to the Thessalonians? Once again, we have an apocalyptic "type scene": the theophany. In verse 16 the Lord comes down from heaven with the traditional Day of the Lord accompaniment of a command, an angelic voice, and God's trumpet.[2] In other words, we do not get just a divine figure arriving here, we get one in full "Day of the Lord" splendor. So what do you suspect should follow such an introduction of a divine figure coming? Nine times out of ten you get cosmic convulsions: the moon should grow dark, the sun shouldn't shine, and stars should start falling. Again, contrary to the usual theophanic procedure, the Lord arrives without cosmic shake-ups to meet first the dead, then the living.

Of course, we should add a caveat here. Paul's letter does not shy away from wrath generally. He speaks about it prior to our text (1 Thess. 1:10; 2:16). It is not that there is no sense of wrath in 1 Thessalonians, but it is telling that Paul does not do it *here* in the middle of his apocalyptic "type scene."

Nonetheless, just by recognizing the form, you have done something important. Had you been doing the normal week-by-week triage that is choosing a lectionary text for Sunday preaching, you might have passed over this one: "too apocalyptic," one might have assumed, "equals too much judgment." But you paused. You were developing your own "eye for the road."

If this book has succeeded in inviting you to pause before passing over an apocalyptic lection, that is great. However, there is more than the occasional speed bump in these texts. They actually offer something "promising." So let us press on.

Set within its proper rhetorical context (4:13–5:11) we begin to get a better picture of what is going on with our little apocalyptic theophany and why Paul has omitted the cosmic convulsions in his use of the form. Rhetorically, the text wants to *do* something with the apocalyptic theophany "type scene." The rhetoric starts in 4:13–14 with the worry about the resurrection and hope for those who "sleep," those whom the community has lost and for whom it grieves. Yet in 5:11, Paul returns to those who "sleep" again, this time actually *destroying* the very concern he answered at the beginning.

Consider closely his words in 5:9–10: "God did not destine us for wrath, but for attaining salvation through our Lord, Jesus Christ, who died for our sake *so that whether awake or asleep* we together might live with him." How did Paul get to a point where he seems to be leveling the very distinction he makes first in favor of those who sleep (they get to rise first to be with the Lord in 4:16), then in favor of those who live "awake" (they are "of the day" in 5:6–8)?

The key is found in the rhetorical arrangement. At the center point of Paul's argument in 5:1 is this little statement: "But as for the times and the seasons, brothers and sisters, you have no need of anything in writing." Now the problem becomes clear. Whether in grieving over the dead in light of eschatological hope or in terms of dealing with remaining faithful in the here and now, a fretting over "times and seasons" in the end is irrelevant to faith. In other words, whether one worries that the dead will "miss out" (4:13–18) or whether one frets over being found faithful before God's new age begins (5:2–5), what is lacking is trust in God. The moment we try to crunch eschatological numbers, we have left the realm of faith. To trust God, by contrast, is precisely to realize that, come what may, God has already given us what we need to face anything: "the breastplate" not of times and seasons, but "faith and love"; and not the "helmet" of the right eschatological timelines, but of "hope of salvation." In that hope, such fretting is superfluous. How do we know? We don't need dispensationalist timetables and slick-haired TV prophecy: we believe in Christ, who has already died and risen (4:14).

In our present context of fear and hype, such a grace-filled word would be quite helpful. We need to do little to summon the fear and hype of the millennium hucksters. Unfortunately, it is already in the awareness of our hearers. What we need to do ultimately in our preaching is to remember good Christology. At the center of God's revelation to us is Christ, who lived and died like us and rose to inaugurate a new age, one marked by not eschatological fretting, but trust in a God who through Christ makes all things new. Given such freedom from "times and seasons," it is also not hard to focus on something more important: "encouraging each other" and "building each other up" (notice their rhetorical prominence at the end of the two parts of the text at 4:18 and 5:11).

So what do you know? We started with anxious grief and the hype of eschatological timetables and ended up with neighbor love. Perhaps that was God's will all along. When you think about it, perhaps that is what our Sunday sermons can do, too.

Spotting Apocalyptic Symbols for Our Homiletical Hermeneutic: Matthew 28:1–10 (Easter A)

This time let's try a text a little off the beaten path of what we normally consider apocalyptic lections. We contended earlier that apocalyptic materials show up in some surprising places. Consider the Matthean text for Easter Sunday and see whether you pick up on any apocalyptic symbols (or maybe even a form).

> [28:1] After the Sabbath, as the first day of the week was dawning, Mary Magdalene and the other Mary came to see the tomb. [2] Just then there was a great earthquake, for an angel of the Lord had come down from heaven, and when he arrived he rolled the stone away and sat upon it. [3] His appearance was like lightning and his clothing white like snow. [4] Those who were guarding trembled from fear of him and they became like dead men. [5] The angel responded by saying to the women, "Do not be afraid, for I know that you are looking for Jesus who was crucified. [6] He is not here, for he was raised just as he said. Come, see the place where he lay. [7] Go quickly and tell his disciples that he is risen from the dead and goes before you to Galilee; there you shall see him. There, I have told you. [8] And they departed quickly from the tomb with fear and great joy and ran to announce the news to his disciples. [9] Then all of a sudden Jesus met them saying, "Greetings!" And they came to him and held on to his feet and worshiped him. [10] Then Jesus said to them, "Do not be afraid; go announce the news to my brothers that they can go to Galilee and see me there."

Did your eyes help you catch anything remotely apocalyptic in our Easter text? This one is a little harder, but offers something worth the effort.

We begin by laying a little groundwork for what we can find there symbolically and generically. Since we are working with a narrative text, our focus will be less on rhetoric and more on genre. Still, the boundaries of the narrative give us some idea of a homiletical destination. Mary Magdalene and Mary go to "see" the tomb, but by the end of the story not only see the risen Christ but also find themselves charged to tell the disciples so that they might see him, too, in Galilee. Some see in order to tell. They, however, tell so that hearers might see.

Shifting now to matters of genre, we discover something interesting. The form in 28:1–10 looks like a second cousin to our throne-room vision form. Rest assured, it is definitely *not* a throne-room vision. Matthew 28:1–10 does not happen in the heavenly throne room at all. However, throne-room visions are probably related to another form that is influential here: call and commissioning narratives. That's where we get stories like Moses and the burning bush. What is interesting, however, is that this resurrection commissioning scene seems to combine some features of both forms. The setting is earthly, as in a typical commissioning, but the symbols surrounding it are cosmic in scope: an angel like lightning dressed in bright-white clothes, a rolling tomb-boulder, an earthquake, and above all, a *resurrection*. In other words, we have before us neither a throne-room vision nor your run-of-the-mill commissioning narrative. We have, rather, a kind of symbolic commissioning narrative. And many of those symbols are of the apocalyptic variety.

Did you catch the apocalyptic symbols? There they were, lurking right there in our Easter A Gospel lection. We usually think of apocalyptic texts as an Advent problem. But perhaps Ernst Käsemann was right that "apocalyptic was the mother of all Christian theology," for we have spotted apocalyptic symbols in this most central element of Christian proclamation: the Easter story.[3]

Why apocalyptic theology? How else can you talk about resurrection in the first century C.E.? We moderns frequently think (and preach) as if resurrection were good news only for individuals dealing with individual death. Biblical texts, however, realize that the good news is of a social and cosmic order, that is, apocalyptic news. The resurrection is about the dawn of the new age. Christ is risen. Now his resurrection is the "first fruits," the sign that God is completing God's intentions in new creation. The resurrection commissioning narratives, like Matthew's, are probably not in the business of reporting earthquakes and trembling Roman guards for purely individualistic and therapeutic reasons. Such social and cosmic symbols are there because resurrection is not so much about just me, but about us in our world. The resurrection marks the beginning of the new creation. No wonder that the ground quakes and Rome's graveyard guards get shook up!

Yet if you are still not sure about the centrality of apocalyptic symbols in an Easter story, think back to Matthew's portrayal of Jesus' death in

27:45–56. Is there something apocalyptically symbolic about Matthew's crucifixion story, too?

It's hard to imagine. After all, in our culture we frequently turn Lent, Holy Week, and the whole mystery of the cross into "Woe is me,"—as if the crucifixion were just a means for evoking a wallowing in personal guilt.

But look again at how Matthew presents the scene symbolically. Sure, there is enough guilt to go around for every human being and every human institution. From the garden to the foot of the cross all our hands get dirty. However, the scene doesn't stop there. As Jesus is dying, darkness falls over all the earth (Matt. 27:45). Bad weather? Probably not. An authorial projection of bad feelings? Doubtful. The image is trying to arrest our attention symbolically using apocalyptic language and the Day of the Lord tradition about the darkening sun (Amos 8:9). The implication? The cross is not just about my sin—although it is that, too—it is about the end of a social, symbolic world. At the cross, our symbolic world begins to die.

That's why Matthew also goes to great pains to include something more in 27:52: "The tombs were opened and many bodies of the saints who had fallen asleep were raised and came out from the tombs after his resurrection, entered the holy city, and appeared to many." Again, these materials are not included in the crucifixion story to enhance their therapeutic value for individuals or even to heighten personal, Lenten guilt. For Matthew the cross is the turning point of the ages. The only way to get at that in Matthew's world, whether at the cross or the empty tomb, is to use symbols of social and cosmic import: *apocalyptic* symbols.

How do you pull that off homiletically? Let us think through the text's form and symbols theologically. You might start where your congregation already has been. We go to the tomb expecting death. Yet we also know that death is more than just biology, a sudden ceasing of the heart or collapse of the lungs. Death is also a power by which humanity is kept in bondage. Abroad, my own U.S. government uses death to control the unruly masses who threaten its economic interests. At home, my own U.S. government uses death within the prison execution system in disproportionate numbers by race. But get this: with Christ those deathly powers have met their match. Rome's guards quaked when the stone was rolled away. After all, without the fear of death, Rome had no more trump cards to control the masses. Now we, therefore, are free to live beyond deathly fear. Sure, we still die. But we can lean into a different kind of future when we trust that death is on the run. Perhaps that's why some, even in the presence of deathly forces of the status quo, still marched in civil rights struggles singing, "We shall overcome some day." They trusted, while standing in death's now receding shadow. Just like Mary Magdalene and Mary, they saw and told. And they told, so others could see, too.

Spotting Apocalyptic Rhetoric for a Homiletical Destination: Revelation 21:1–6 (New Year ABC, All Saints B, Easter 5C)

With this text we now push our newly developed "eyes for the road" in the most challenging way. See, however, if you can begin discerning what this text is *doing* simply by reading it. Where in the world is its rhetoric going?

[21:1] And I saw a new heaven and a new earth; for the first heaven and the first earth passed away, and the sea was no more.

[2] And I saw the holy city, new Jerusalem, coming down from heaven from God, prepared as a bride adorned for her husband.

[3] And I heard a loud voice from the throne saying, "Behold, the dwelling of God is with people, and he shall dwell with them; and they shall be his people, and God himself shall be with them, [4] and he shall wipe away every tear from their eyes, and death shall not be any more. Neither suffering, nor crying, nor pain shall be any more, because the first things passed away."

[5] And the one seated on the throne said, "Behold, I make all things new." And he said, "Write, for these words are faithful and true." [6] And he said to me, "It is finished. I am the A and the Z, the beginning and the end." (author's translation)

So what is this text doing? It gives a few oral cues and directions that can begin guiding us toward a "destination" for our sermons.

First, the vision starts in 21:1 with a description that passes from the old to the new creation. The section begins with an oral directional cue: "Then I saw."

The same cue seems to mark the beginning of the second section in verse 2. Now, however, the object of the vision shifts to the new Jerusalem.

With the third section, 21:3–4, the means of identifying the movement shifts from what is seen to what is heard from the throne. We have seen a cosmic vision, but now the voice from the throne (and not just some angel as in most apocalypses) interprets what this means: an end of crying, pain, and death. Why? Because the first things have passed away.

With the final section, 21:5–6, the voice from the throne is heard again. Now, however, both the vision (sections 1 and 2) and the promised outcome for humanity (section 3) are vouched for in the person of the One seated on the throne. The vision and its promises reside in the one who is A and Z, beginning and end. Why is this important? At the beginning we learned that the old creation passed away, the new creation began. However, this was no divine afterthought. God is in God's self first and last, beginning and end.

This also leads to a second rhetorical insight about our text. We need to consider *who* is doing the action throughout this text. God is the subject of just about every verb. We, by contrast, are not the ultimate agents of new creation. We simply overhear the vision that John relates.

This does not mean, of course, that human action is unrelated to new creation. We have a role to play, especially as the recipients of such wonderful divine promises from the throne. Revelation 21 indicates as much by noting in verses 7–8 that human unfaithfulness is problematic. The new creation is God's doing, but that does not ultimately leave us without a call to faithfulness.

Nonetheless, this vision by its very focus on God's action highlights something very important for us as we deal with apocalyptic texts. In the end, the vision is fulfilled *as an act of divine grace*.

On the surface, the notion of apocalyptic grace is hard to believe. Many think of apocalyptic texts as somehow sub-Christian; too much works, not enough grace; too much violence, not enough peace. In reality, however, apocalyptic texts participate in the same kind of ambiguity as other biblical texts. Many kinds of texts do contain puzzling episodes of violence and sometimes say things that seem less than grace-full. Martin Luther, in discerning justification by grace through faith as the center of the gospel, could then question whether James was "an epistle of straw" or Revelation belonged in the canon at all. The problem is indeed there, but actually broader than just apocalyptic texts.

We have seen, however, that designations that dismiss apocalyptic texts as useless or sub-Christian were not always borne out as we engaged our texts. After all, here in Revelation 21:1–6, precisely *after* several chapters of some of the worst apocalyptic carnage, we discover that this text wishes to do something grace-full. While the struggle and the violence of Revelation are awful and frequently problematic for us, the vision here serves as a grace-filled light at the end of the tunnel. In the end, even this text chooses to draw us forward with grace, to lure us into God's new creation on the basis of God's desire to wipe away tears.

If you are still not sure, all you have to do is ask the same question of a genre analysis of the text. Is there any other evidence that would persuade us that this text is about God's grace in new creation? Rest assured, this vision of the new creation in Revelation 20—21 is not the only one in apocalyptic literature. By studying a couple of others, the uniquely grace-oriented approach of Revelation 21:1–6 comes into even greater relief. The passages set side by side show what they have in common and how they differ.

Rev. 20:11–21:8 (Final Vision, Last Half)	*1 Enoch* 45:2–6 (*Similitudes*)	*1 Enoch* 91:12–17 (*Apocalypse of Weeks*)
1. Judge is seated on a great white throne	1. Judgment of sinners and deniers of the Lord of Spirits	1. Righteous (Judges) do judgment on oppressors
2. Universal judgment of dead, Death, and Hades	2. Elect One (Judge) is seated on the throne of glory	2. Righteous build a New Temple [Jerusalem?]
3. New heaven, new earth appear; first ones pass away	3. The elect who appeal to God's name will stand firm	3. Sin departs and is judged; uprightness triumphs
4. New Jerusalem comes down from heaven	4. God causes elect one to dwell among them	4. First heaven passes away; New Heaven comes
5. God dwells among them	5. New Heaven, New Earth	5. Heaven shines forever
6. The faithless are punished	6. Righteous dwell before God; sinners destroyed forever	6. Righteousness shall last forever; sin is just a memory

With the texts above we learn what is communicatively unique about Revelation 21:1–6. First, unlike *1 Enoch* 91, Revelation's righteous do not seem to share in judging sinners (cf. 20:4–6). Second, the appearance of the new creation represents the fourth or fifth element in Enoch's apocalypses, while in Revelation it comes earlier. Third, Revelation's vision of the new creation and Jerusalem/Temple is not ultimately dependent on human action (e.g., building temples, or upright living) as it is in *1 Enoch* 91. In Revelation 20:11–21:8 all the action, from judgment to salvific vision, is God's. Though human beings are called to be faithful at the end (see 21:7–8), the salvific vision is itself pure gift of God.

Having confirmed by means of the text's rhetoric and genre how the vision orients to God's grace-filled action, we now can see how some of the symbols work. The vision seems to stand as it does at the end of struggle. It offers, as Revelation 5 did, an alternative vision of our world that calls forth action. This is *hypomone,* "steadfast resistance," to the powers that be.

Such an understanding of Revelation 21's symbolic world is, however, problematic for us who tend to be more comfortable than not. While many of us experience oppression by virtue of gender, race, or sexual orientation, many of us do not. How do we interpret this symbolic world for the comfortable?

It is important to remember that we ourselves are also buffeted about by the cosmic forces of systemic evil. Such evil often benefits us (e.g., cheap banana prices), yet it demands untoward sacrifices from us, too. While we who live in first-world comfort cannot take the mantle of victimization too quickly, we do live in a world where only one person can be "top dog." In the great pyramid of power that is late, Western, *laissez faire* global capitalism, we are situated some small, relative distance down. Our sacrifice is relatively small and comfort laden. In exchange for a middle-class lifestyle, so the tacit agreement goes, we won't scream too loudly when others suffer injustice further down the pyramid. The problem is this: in the meantime we forget the humanity of the people worse off than we *and* we even "forget" our own. Can the vision pierce the numbness? Perhaps.

In the end, however, it is important to remember what the vision is *doing,* where it is heading. At the end of the vision stands not a stripped down humanity of righteous and unrighteous individuals, but a God who seeks communion with us: "Behold, the dwelling of God is with people, and he shall dwell with them; and they shall be his people, and God himself shall be with them." Our neighbors and our humanity are not discardable, they are what God desires to commune with, both some day and this day.

This means, by the way, that this vision is preached with more than some sweet "some day" in view. The vision exists to interpret our present reality and to call us to action in the here and now. Sermons should rightly begin with the experiences of chaos, pain, and crying we know today. Take care not to exhaust that pain with our personal realities. A sermon that deals with the cosmic scope of this vision should also deal with the economic and political realities that tear us apart from our neighbors. In the end, however, a sermon, like the rhetoric of the vision, must turn to the promise of no more tears and crying. If the sermon is done well, the promise will grow precisely out of the suffering. The vision does not bypass tears, it wipes them away. The difference for a plausibly believable gospel sermon is like night and day. Even then, however, the sermon doesn't end until it reaches the throne. The vision is not ours to build, it is the gift of God. Yet, as gift, it does not call forth passivity, but action. Preachers will want to note those places where the gift or a promise frees us to act in ways we could not have done if left to our own devices.

CONCLUSION

It is fitting that we should end here. We have been dealing with a vision that, though a gift, calls us to action.

The problem, as pastors are well aware, is that we live in a fearful time. The millennial hype works only because the church is already scared of the present, not to speak of the future. Why? Many people quote the King James Version of Proverbs 29:18, "Where there is no vision, the people perish." In our day, however, the thought could be rephrased: "Where there is no vision, the people *parish*." For fear of the world, we frequently trade our visionary hope for a mess of pottage: church growth schemes, the latest management technique, or settling for a warmed-over therapeutic personalism that reduces the world, and the gospel that should be addressing it, to my little feelings.

At times like this, it may be important to remember that it was not always so. More than two centuries ago, John Wesley, who would not be confined by parish boundaries that often kept the church closed off from the suffering masses, coined an interesting phrase: "The world is my parish." The thought is a useful one. There are some who would have us circle the wagons against the world's onslaughts. For them the church has its own language, its own story, perhaps even its own world. Yet one thing we must by now have noted with great consistency. In the apocalyptic texts we have considered, the new creation is *bigger* than the church. The church may be its vanguard, it may even have something important to say to the world; however, the church does not have the option of hunkering down behind cultural fences, doors of exclusion, or even in the most beautiful of stained-glass realities.

So now we've come full circle. Do you remember the stained-glass window of the new Jerusalem? Through it you saw, overlaying our broken world, a vision of something new. As a purely aesthetic object for the people inside alone, the vision would seem to leave our world intact. As a vision overlaying our reality, however, and prompting our gaze outward, it can both grace us with its promise and convey a call to join in the struggle for a world where such brokenness, whether within the church or without, is a memory.

I have heard that the Inuit people of the Arctic North have twenty-eight words for snow. If that is true, it would seem to indicate something useful for us to consider, too. The Inuit can see more kinds of snow than most of us are able to see. What a marvelous gift! Yet even this "seeing" is not an end in itself. Why should a culture need to have twenty-eight words for snow, if not to be graced to deal with each kind? It may be, for example, that certain kinds of snow are suitable for walking on, some for tracking food, and some for building homes. In other words, the ability to see with the eyes of such a vision promptly draws us *through* the vision to the world and the latent possibilities for communion with God and neighbor in it.

There's a church in East Nashville that has long struggled with both its vision and its place in the world. Historically, they have been a white church in a transitional neighborhood. When the time came that most of the members had moved out of the neighborhood, they could have packed it up as many big, inner-city churches have done, and headed for the relative safety of the suburbs. What is odd is that they did not. No doubt, the reasons for such decisions are complex: what cause elicited what effect in that choice is not simple to discern. Yet I cannot help but remember one thing about that church that I noticed whenever I preached there. When standing at the pulpit, you look out through a stained-glass window of Jesus the Good Shepherd. As you do, you see Jesus tending the flock in the now "transitional" neighborhood of the church. Mind you, its location still is an ongoing issue for the congregation. Every church is a product of its social class and glorious 1950s history, so decisions about the building and access and what happens there are never easy. Nonetheless, this church opens its doors on more than one occasion each week to inner-city children and recovering alcoholics. After a recent tornado, the church became a base for church members and national disaster relief agency people to go out and check on what their neighbors needed. When I look out from the pulpit through the stained-glass window, I have to wonder. Perhaps it is easier to stay, to fling open the doors, and once in a while even to venture outside to the world, when you know Jesus, the Good Shepherd, has gone out ahead of you.

Therefore, in the end, our little human words from the pulpit only matter because God has already spoken and already gotten things going. Perhaps we can preach in the new creation, because God has already started: by offering a vision, bidding us to live *through* it, and inviting us to join God in the world. How did the One seated on the throne put it? "Behold," God says, "Behold, I make all things new."

---

1. Again, with 1 Thess. 4:13–5:11 I have translated not just for the eye, but for the ear: e.g., the words for "bereft" and "rest" in 4:13 have similar consonants in Greek (λυπῆσθε and λοιποὶ). Hence, the unusual word choice.

2. J. Plevnik offers an excellent tradition-critical study of these motifs as they appear in our text, "The *Parousia* as Implications of Christ's Resurrection (An Exegesis of 1 Thes 4:13–18)," in *Word and Spirit,* ed. J. Plevnik (Willowdale, Ont.: Regis College Press, 1975), esp. 234–51.

3. Ernst Käsemann, "The Beginnings of Christian Theology," in *Apocalypticism,* ed. R. Funk (New York: Herder & Herder, 1969), 40.

Appendix 1:
Resources for the Apocalyptic Preacher

Biblical Resources

Apocalyptic Materials in Pauline Texts

Beker, J. Christiaan. *Paul's Apocalyptic Gospel*. Philadelphia: Fortress, 1982.
———. *The Triumph of God*. Minneapolis: Fortress, 1990.
> Both these books can be useful to preachers wrestling with how apocalyptic thinking informs Pauline texts. The first tries to interpret Paul for the church today. The second is a thorough yet compact overview of Paul's apocalyptic theology.

Brown, Alexandra. *The Cross and Human Transformation: Paul's Apocalyptic Word in 1 Corinthians*. Minneapolis: Fortress, 1995.
> A fine study of how apocalyptic thinking informs Paul's understanding of the cross.

Käsemann, Ernst. *Commentary on Romans*. Grand Rapids: Eerdmans, 1980.
———. *Perspectives on Paul*. Philadelphia: Fortress, 1971.
> Käsemann called apocalyptic the mother of Christian theology. These books are classic and still useful for Paul's apocalyptic texts.

Books on Revelation

Fiorenza, Elisabeth Schüssler. *Revelation: Vision of a Just World*. Minneapolis: Fortress, 1991.
> A great literary-rhetorical and historical commentary for getting at the liberating *and* oppressive dimensions of Revelation.

Pippin, Tina. *Death and Desire: The Rhetoric of Gender in the Apocalypse of John*. Louisville, Ky.: Westminster/John Knox, 1992. This book has, among other things, an honest treatment of Revelation's troubling legacy of gender archetypes: the bride and the whore. It should be read by anyone who wants to rehabilitate Revelation for the contemporary pulpit. The book includes artwork depicting women in Revelation.

Talbert, Charles. *The Apocalypse: A Reading of the Revelation of John.* Louisville, Ky.: Westminster John Knox, 1994.

Talbert offers a literary perspective while offering several cross-references to parallel texts in Jewish apocalypses and other sources. This commentary can be useful for further research into apocalyptic texts.

Resources for Your Own Apocalyptic Interpretation

Basic Reference for Noncanonical Apocalyptic Texts

Charlesworth, James, ed. *The Old Testament Pseudepigrapha.* 2 vols. New York: Doubleday, 1983.

The first volume contains most everything you will need to study Jewish apocalypses and related literature. The marginal notes make it easy to use for cross-references to biblical texts.

Reddish, Mitchell G., ed. *Apocalyptic Literature: A Reader.* Peabody, Mass.: Hendrickson, 1995.

Reddish has many of the same translations of apocalypses as volume 1 of *The Old Testament Pseudepigrapha.* The advantage is that it is much cheaper; the disadvantage, less background and fewer notes for research.

Apocalyptic Texts and Genre Analysis

Collins, John J. *The Apocalyptic Imagination.* 2d ed. Grand Rapids: Eerdmans, 1998.

The book is demanding, yet it summarizes well the trends of research in apocalyptic literature.

———. *Daniel; with an Introduction to Apocalyptic Literature.* Grand Rapids: Eerdmans, 1984.

This book is great for its glossary of apocalyptic forms insofar as they are found in Daniel.

———. ed. *Apocalypse: The Morphology of a Genre. Semeia* 14. Missoula, Mont.: Scholars, 1979.

This book is good, but you really have to love apocalyptic literature—not for the fainthearted!

Yarbro Collins, Adela, ed. *Early Christian Apocalypticism: Genre and Social Setting. Semeia* 36. Decatur, Ga.: Scholars, 1986.

This book pushes aspects of the genre debate beyond the definition developed by the original Apocalypse Group of the Society of Biblical Literature Genres Project. Some contributions are demanding; most are insightful.

Rhetorical Analysis and What Texts *Do*

Kennedy, George. *New Testament Interpretation through Rhetorical Criticism.* Chapel Hill: Univ. of North Carolina Press, 1984.
> An excellent place to begin for those who wish to try rhetorical criticism of New Testament texts.

Mack, Burton. *Rhetoric and the New Testament.* Minneapolis: Fortress, 1990.
> This offers helpful background to rhetorical studies in the New Testament.

Symbol Analysis and Social Worlds

Berger, Peter. *The Sacred Canopy.* Garden City, N.Y.: Doubleday, 1967.

Berger, Peter, and Thomas Luckmann. *The Social Construction of Reality: A Treatise on the Sociology of Knowledge.* New York: Doubleday, 1966.
> These books are surprisingly fun reading. Berger loves theological types (see his Appendix 2 for theologians in *The Sacred Canopy,* 179–85).

Preaching

Collections of Sermons on Apocalyptic Texts

Boesak, Allan. *Comfort and Protest: The Apocalypse from a South African Perspective.* Philadelphia: Westminster, 1987.
> These sermons will help you understand why and how John's Apocalypse can be liberating.

Rogers, Cornish, and Joey Jeter, eds. *Preaching through the Apocalypse.* St. Louis, Mo.: Chalice, 1992.
> Like most sermon collections, this is a little uneven. Nonetheless, the diversity of sermons will spur you to consider how you might do it.

Homiletics and Apocalyptic Texts

Buttrick, David. *The Mystery and the Passion.* Minneapolis: Fortress, 1992.

———. *Preaching Jesus Christ.* Philadelphia: Fortress, 1988.

———. *Preaching the New and the Now.* Louisville, Ky.: Westminster John Knox, 1998.
> Buttrick has a great appreciation for apocalyptic texts. His exegesis is careful and challenging. The images he spins out as he interprets them may help you to go and do likewise in your preaching.

Craddock, Fred. "Preaching the Book of Revelation." *Interpretation* 40, no. 3 (1986): 270–82.
> Craddock's article is helpful and thoughtful for preachers who truly wrestle with Revelation.

Long, Thomas G. "The Preacher and the Beast: From Apocalyptic Text to Sermon." In *Intersections: Post-Critical Studies in Preaching,* ed. Richard Eslinger. Grand Rapids: Eerdmans, 1994.
Long's brilliant chapter in this book challenges our perceptions of Revelation by helping us consider its form and how to preach it.

Appendix 2:
Sample Sermons on Apocalyptic Texts

On the following pages are three sermons based on the apocalyptic lectionary texts treated in detail in chapters 2 through 6. They are included for those who still wonder what a sermon on a New Testament apocalyptic text might be like. Yet they have been placed in the relative remoteness of an appendix lest they prematurely short-circuit any reader's own homiletical engagement with apocalyptic texts. As a teacher of preaching, I trust that they will serve not as an invitation to imitation but as a call to go and do likewise—rather, to go and do *better*. Discerning readers will note, of course, that the sermons included here betray something of their time and place. Yet that is not all bad. Perhaps then even my modest and dated efforts can inspire you in your own time and place—in your own way—to preach in the new creation.

Sermon 1

Homiletical Rationale

We discerned in chapter 2 that the rhetoric of a text can show us "where in the world we are going" in our sermons. The rhetoric of Mark 13:24–37 does so by evoking a change in the way we "watch." The sermon below therefore moves from a sense of "watching in anxiety" in the picture of a cathedral ceiling painting of Christ's return to an active watching that takes its cue from the grace God demonstrates in the Christ who came and comes again. In other words, the sermon's "destination" is a grace-based "active watching" in engagement with our world.

We noted in chapter 3 that the form of the sermon helps us figure out "how in the world we will get there." The apocalyptic form we discovered in Mark 13:24–27, the apocalyptic theophany, surprised us by giving us something other than the expected apocalyptic blood bath. Rather than coming in judgment, Christ comes on the clouds solely to "gather the elect." The route of our sermon, therefore, passes through a fear of judgment to a realization of divine mercy.

In chapter 4 we saw that symbols don't just reflect a prior reality, but sometimes evoke a new one or tear down an old one. In this way a text's apocalyptic symbols can show us "what in the world we will see along the way" in our sermons. The symbols Mark 13:24–37 offers depict a world "falling apart," that is, a world being "delegitimized." This sermon, therefore, allows that symbolic world to help interpret those places in our symbolic reality that are "falling apart" and views them not just as problems but as occasions or signs for discerning God's strangely wide mercy.

Sermon Text: Mark 13:24–37 (Advent 1B)

Title: My Lord, What a Morning, When the Stars Begin to Fall!

There's a cathedral in Europe with a massive painting of the second coming of Christ across the ceiling. You know, one of those huge, multicolored murals with Jesus returning to judge. His eyes are blazing fire; his feet, planted on a cloud. He's ready to give it to sinners. Below, human figures are painted along the ceiling's edge. Their faces are contorted in terror.

Mark's Gospel paints a scary picture for *us* too. The world depicted here is chaotic: stars careen downward; sun, moon are made dark. The very powers of the heavens reel from shaking. And all we can do is witness the scene, drop-jawed in fear. The world is collapsing upon us. And we are rightly afraid.

I

No doubt our world *is* being shaken. The ground virtually quakes beneath our feet. Our established world seems to be toppling over. Just take a stroll through an inner-city neighborhood. Go out for a walk on city streets to look at our tumble-down world. Sure, you might spot a few renovated homes dotting the block in an old blue-collar part of town. But now look between those manicured lawns at the burnt-out shells of old one-family houses, torched for insurance cash. And don't forget to check up the street. A few houses away you might see an African-American family moving out of the new public housing duplex next door. Apparently their white neighbors weren't too happy about them living there. Houses getting fixed up, others burnt down; folks moving in; others run out. People call it a "transitional neighborhood." It seems more like a world in chaos. Of course, you can always cut short your neighborhood walk. But just try to cocoon in your home to keep the chaos locked out—there's no escape. Just flip on your TV set to the news reports, and you get Bosnia flashing across your living room TV screen. Serbian forces rock Sarajevo with shells from the hills. Muslims snipe from burnt-out skyscrapers, trying to pick off Serbian artillery crews. Meanwhile UN armored vehicles rumble through the Bosnian countryside, ferrying a truckload of gaunt-cheeked refugees on the return trip. Nobody, not even the well-coiffed reporter, can tell you what the outcome will be, whether union, semi-autonomous regions, or mob rule. So you yank out the TV cord—just to get that chaos shut off! We may try to cocoon away in our comfortable home, but the world's chaos still manages to press inside. Then comes the last line of defense. You plop in your Lazyboy recliner, switch on the soft lamplight, and curl up to read a glossy magazine about nature. You page past the wilderness cover, flip through the Sierra Club ads, and what do you find but article after article about ozone depletion or the greenhouse effect. Leafing toward the back cover, you spot a street-level photo spread on L.A. smog. From your vantage point all you can see in the photo is a gray-brown blanket shrouding the city skyline. No sun, no moon peeking through at night. Just a tumbledown world. Try as you may, there's no avoiding the chaos. You see, we're living in a creation on the edge of collapse. Our world's falling apart.

II

So no wonder we see gavel-down judgment coming. We spy disaster on the horizon. We expect a kind of reckoning for our world. Of course, we may be a little skeptical about out-and-out *judgment*. After all, we've all grown up mouthing platitudes about acceptance. "I'm OK, you're OK," we say, "as long as we keep a be happy attitude, we can keep those negative vibes at bay." But while we mouth the words, deep down don't we also fear a reckoning's at hand? We've become like little children playing at home in a living room chock-full of treasured knickknacks. We're not supposed to play so rough, but—kids will be kids—in no time we're running around roughhousing again. Suddenly the freewheeling gets out of hand. A porcelain vase topples off the shelf. A precious gift, an heirloom, shatters on the floor. Our playmates fall silent. All we can hear are ever-quickening parental steps echoing louder and louder on the kitchen tiles. We know

125

what's coming down. The thing's broken. It's judgment time. So now, grown up, we're being forced to deal with our consumer excess, two decades of binge and spend, binge and spend even more. Oh, our recent opulence has made for a great bash, but now the bills are mounting. And the poor—why, the ragtag mass of homeless just keeps burgeoning. We'd like to think there's no connection between our wealth and their need. But the empty-handed, starving army grows while they keep rapping on the windshields of our cars, one palm out pressing us for bread. Deep inside we must know that the whole thing's broken and the clock's struck judgment time. We know a verdict's coming down. We live in fear of judgment.

III

But get a look at who is coming to judge: Jesus! "His honor" is Mercy himself. The one charged with our judgment is forgiveness-in-the-flesh, Jesus Christ. Of course, who else would you want for a judge? We've heard of him cavorting with outcasts, eating bread among untouchables, hoisting a few with the dregs. Why, he's just the kind of person you'd want for a judge. We know all the stories of Jesus absolving sinners, too, healing folks right under the noses of lawyers. We've even watched Jesus on the cross, the place of his own judgment. "Forgive them," Jesus says, "forgive them." It seems this Jesus who's been judged just *will not judge*. No wonder, then, that Jesus' end-time appearance leaves us shocked. We see clouds on the horizon and expect judgment. But Humanity's Child coasts in on a cumulus not to zap sinners but to gather all the elect from one end of the earth to the other. Jesus returns cloud-footed in apocalyptic splendor, and contrary to accustomed judicial procedure, to accomplish our final liberation. You see, Jesus "the Judge" comes solely to save. Imagine that! At the end of all things stands Jesus Christ, all but decked out in a judicial robe, yet for the express purpose of dispensing mercy. Well, perhaps some people's names just don't fit their appointed tasks at first hearing. Maybe there are folks whose monikers do not sound appropriate to their titles at first blush. You know, like "Doctor Bill" or perhaps "Reverend Grace." But maybe there is one appellation good enough, one odd-as-God combination worth considering: How about a judge who goes by the name of mercy! Imagine standing before the bar of that justice's court. The whole world's gathered there, slumped down before the bench of judgment. Then the bailiff cries: "All rise! All rise!" she says, "Judge Mercy presiding!" Just think of that. Jesus Christ pronounces acquittal over us. Our judge is mercy.

IV

Well, we should have seen it coming! After all, we Christian folk have caught at least a glimpse of Christ's new age with our own eyes. Surely we of all people have seen a new world taking shape already. Just look around and you'll spy God's new creation emerging out of the rubble of our world. Remember the story of the Berlin Wall coming down? For some time East German churches had been providing "free space," public forums for airing grievances among an otherwise voiceless people. But before long the church buildings in places like Dresden and Leipzig could not contain the spiritual power welled up within them. Energized in the churches, people started marching in cobblestone streets. Then, before the soldiers on either side of the razor-spiked wall could blink, the barricade came tumbling down. The khaki-colored military folk on both sides could only stand by and watch while graffiti-covered sections of the wall got sliced away. With the military razor wire cut, folks scrambled up on top. Then amid the wreckage of the old divided world the German people danced. Now that was a sign: folks kicking up their heels on the rubble of the age! But turn now and consider ourselves. We might also be aware of a new world of mercy taking shape among us already right here in communion. After all, every so often we Christian folk leave our pews, walk down the aisle, and whet our appetites with a little Lord's Supper. There we kneel at the rail, rubbing shoulders with the dangdest people, sinners all. In spite of the old world's divisions, we become part of Christ's new creation of mercy. All we need's a little broken bread, some wine poured out—and suddenly a sign: mercy incarnate! Barriers between us come tumbling down. Suddenly sinners are on the mend—together! How does the old spiritual go? "My Lord, what a morning; My Lord, what a morning; My Lord, what a morning, when the stars begin to fall!" Well no wonder the old spiritual is so upbeat. Sure, for some folks falling stars could mean only the deepest night. But the spiritual calls us to sing a different tune. In the midst of chaos, look for God's new creation. When the stars do fall, well, a new morning is at hand. No wonder folks can sing "My Lord, what a morning, when the stars begin to fall!" Can you see it? The new age has already begun breaking in before our eyes. In bits and pieces we too catch a glimpse of Christ's new world.

V

So now the key's to stay awake. We don't want to miss the dawning of a new day! We have to keep hands and feet moving, watching for Christ's new world. Perhaps what we need is to start "watching like a waitress." People waiting tables know to keep busy while they watch for someone to stroll through the restaurant doors. What do you do? Maybe you fold the silverware into cloth napkins. Then look out the window to check who's coming to dinner. Make sure to fill the sugar bowl, top off the seasonings, and pour on the cream. Then be sure to scan your tables to see if anybody's pulling up a chair. You see, a waitress does have to keep an eye out for folks who might be hungry. But no matter what, a waitress keeps busy while watching. After all, you never know when you might have a banquet on your hands. At any moment the feast might begin. Then you need to keep the food coming, piping hot plate after plate. Let the wine flow like rivers because everybody's going to get their fill of the cup. But for the moment, just keep your eyes peeled while you do what God requires. "Watch like a waitress." What was it old Martin Luther said? If he knew the world were ending tomorrow, he'd plant a tree. Well, that is fine as far as it goes, but why not be a little more imaginative? Perhaps we church folk can keep plugging away at whatever it is we do. We might be putting our hands to work in our dilapidated neighborhoods, improving housing not just for yuppies but for the poor. Perhaps some of us set our feet to marching on the streets so that even the homeless might share a little bread. Whatever it is—keep at it. Lean into the wind, anticipating that God's new creation is just around the corner. So keep your feet moving, your hands busy. You won't want to miss out on Christ's new world. Keep watching for the new creation.

So here we are, called to be ready for the new thing God is doing. Who needs to watch anxiously for some blazing-eyed Judge? We're getting mercy! Now we are free to keep our eyes peeled for new creation. In the meantime, keep stepping out in faith. After all, God has big plans for our world—and we've seen just the beginning.

Sermon 2

Homiletical Rationale

In chapter 5 we learned that the rhetoric of Revelation 5 was trying to "expand the cast," that is, to invite the hearers and all creation into a realization of their liberated destiny as royalty and priests. This sermon moves toward that understanding by using a dramatic metaphor. The introduction starts at a movie theater and adopts the point of view of spectators. By the end, however, we realize that we are "part of the cast" and invited into God's paschal plot. So "Lights, camera . . ." There, you said it: action.

We learned about the throne-room vision form in apocalypses, the unique way in which John the seer used the form to help us determine a "route" for our sermons. We called it "christological inversion": from the lion to the Lamb. This sermon therefore plots its movement similarly. It starts from a sensed need for a bigger-than-life messianic figure to help us cope with the chaos of contemporary life. In the middle, however, we realize that the Lamb standing though slain (Christ crucified yet risen) is the sign of our coming paschal liberation. Freedom does not come through our cultural demigods: Hollywood Terminator-types, Wall Street's "masters of the universe," or might-makes-right military heroes. The path to freedom, like the route of our sermon, passes through the cross of Christ.

Our symbol analysis also provided us with "signs to see along the way." In the case of Revelation 5 it had to do with the maintenance of an "alternative world." This symbolic reality, while not allowing us to simply wish our world away, becomes an occasion for us to realize that even our world is not "fixed" or eternal. For this sermon, therefore, it will be necessary to play with different realities "interacting" and interpreting one another. The dramatic metaphor will help. Where stage and audience meet, worlds collide. Using this metaphor for the sermon will function as a hermeneutical tool for preaching. Sometimes we change the world. Sometimes a world changes us. Apocalyptic and contemporary symbols can help a sermon do the work that the text intends.

Sermon Text: Revelation 5:1–14 (Easter 3C)

Title: Now for the Royal Finale: "Lights, Camera, . . . "

The film *The Purple Rose of Cairo* portrays a couple of Depression-era women spending their spare time watching the movies. It doesn't matter what's on the marquee. They're only there to escape Depression drear. Yet one day the whole theater is thrown into chaos. Some characters on screen suddenly start chatting with our moviegoers in their seats. Before long, two disgruntled characters quit the film. They refuse to go on with the show. Absent two characters, the film grinds to a halt. The plot can't continue. It's stuck—mid-frame. Well, perhaps we too live in an age when the future has come to a screeching halt. After all, does any real *news* seem possible, what with a world economy stuck in eternal grind-it-out recession? And how long do we have to keep on watching the same old carnage in Yugoslavia? So we sit passively in our living rooms, eyes glazed over, facing a TV repeating rerun after rerun. Might as well pull the plug. All we've got is the same old same old: a cosmic show stuck in mid-frame.

I

Well, heaven only knows how *our* great drama will end! The conclusion of our human story is a mystery to us. God knows what humanity's final act will be. Oh, we try our best to see through the murky fog of the future, but to no avail. When we wonder about tomorrow's weather, we catch the forecast on TV. But if we pose a specific question, the cumuli begin to gather. Despite all the maps and satellite photos, chances of rain tomorrow are still just cloudy percentages. If we ask forecasters to dispel the meteorological murkiness, they just shrug their shoulders. "Maybe, maybe not." Of course, haziness about the future plagues the church, too. After all, our institutional future is hardly assured. So we call in church growth experts to help us manage the future. They schlepp along charts and prop up their graphs. Then these prognosticators spin out the latest marketing info—demographic data to help the church ensure its future market share. But ask our experts the $64,000 question: "Will the church survive to be faithful?" They can only throw up their hands: "God only knows," they say. It's as if we were caught in the mistiness of some divine Agatha Christie mystery novel. God, like some heavenly Dame Agatha, has plopped us in the middle of a plot. But we characters play our parts utterly without a clue. We haven't the foggiest idea how our complicated plot will unravel. In perfectly good Agatha Christie fashion, we can't even spot the key to its resolution. It's all so murky. Because for us the future's a mystery. The plot's finale is hidden from sight. How will the story end? Heaven only knows.

II

Well perhaps what we need is a star-studded hero to take the stage. You know, some cosmic protagonist to bring the house down. Our world needs some bigger-than-life hero to wrangle out a happy ending! You know the type. You see them at the movies all the time. Matinee idol John Wayne would do, storming blood-speckled beaches under enemy fire. Or how about some big-screen Sigourney Weaver type to single-handedly knock off space aliens—she could do the job right. Or better yet, give the job to movie-star Ronald Reagan, riding a horse into a rough-and-tumble Western town to clean it up. That's what we need! A bigger-than-life hero to steer our world's meandering plot in the right direction. Our world needs . . . a *messiah*. You know, a real tiger. Some cosmic go-getter in a three-piece suit. A member of our country's Wall Street pantheon would do—anyone who has a knack for getting things done. What did author Thomas Wolfe call them—

"Masters of the Universe"? We know the type. They command monster salaries with perks to die for. But these Wall Street titans are worth it. They savage the corporate hierarchy, wringing out wage concessions, and even manage to increase productivity. No wonder we worship the ground they walk on. These messianic demigods of the business world—they know how to get things done. Why one of them's just what we need! Someone to whip our future into shape. So bring on our messiah. Let 'em storm the stage. We want some no-nonsense titan to play the part with messianic gusto.

III

Yet look who God casts for the part: a messianic Lamb. God's hero on the cosmic stage is a sacrificial victim. God's choice for the messiah role— Christ crucified! Now, we must admit, it is hardly the subject of polite conversation. But we do, after all, live in a world that worships health in the sleek-bodied forms of the rich and famous. Our messiahs usually control a wad of cash or dispense power like candy. Sure, Jesus does still have a fairly good image in our culture—high positives, low negatives. Yet he hardly measures up to the heroes who really deliver the goods. There's a suburban church not far from here located in an environment that demonstrates the problem. Sure, the church is a nice-looking building—a little cross out in front, too. But what is telling is what's around it. This church is surrounded by the great representatives of global capitalism. A sleek, new shopping mall on one side, a Wal-Mart superstore on the other. And with that picture in mind, is it hard to imagine whose parking lots are full? In a world of neon signs, fashion mirrors, and the latest consumer goods at discount prices, a little cross just gets crowded out. Of course, the problem is not a new one— it goes back to the very beginning. Maybe that character in the musical *Jesus Christ Superstar* was right. Jesus debuts in his messianic role in the most primitive of times. Oh, there's technology if you count boulders, bronze, maybe a little iron—but no TV back then! And then there's the problem of staging: why, Galilee and Palestine were backwaters. And in the end, what was he? Just another victim on a cross. Yet Jesus is the one whom God casts in the messiah role. God chooses a Lamb for savior of the world. From our world's point of view, hardly a messianic star.

IV

Yet look again: Jesus is following a different redemption script. He performs the messiah role as *Passover Lamb . . . for our sake.* The Lamb's our cue that we belong to God. Through the Lamb we are recast as God's Passover possession! Remember Jesus at his birth scene? A tiny child in a manger, Jesus is helpless, at the mercy of others. Baby Jesus is born in poverty, amid the oppression of his own people under the heavy burden of imperial taxation, the iron bar of Roman rule. He's such a tiny baby for these cruel times! But give him your hand, and his little fingers reach up to hold on tight. This little one, a victim even now, holds your life in his hand and won't let go. Now see Jesus thirty-odd years later against the backdrop of a stormy Jerusalem. He came in peace, but the people have turned against him. Jesus faces an angry crowd bent on stringing up one more victim. Religious leaders hand him over. The political hacks execute their judgment by having Jesus nailed on a wooden cross. But even crucified, Jesus is not just another victim—for three days later Christ is raised. The stone sealed by imperial guards and watched over by religious authorities gets rolled away. The victim is risen! And the result is this: death's icy grip is undone. But the risen Christ, the risen Christ holds on—through life and death and life again. Now catch a glimpse of Jesus in John's heavenly vision finale. In the throne room of heaven the hosts wait to see who will unseal the scroll to get the final act rolling. Who is qualified to do the job? The lion of Judah? The root of mighty King David? No! A little lamb is, *the Lamb* standing though slain. The one who was a victim—and is now at God's right hand, this Jesus is qualified to unveil God's future for us. So look who holds tight to our future in a scroll in his hand: the slaughtered Lamb standing on the throne. Make no mistake, Jesus cues us in on the truth: we belong to God. The Lamb makes us God's Passover possession. Jesus acts as Passover Lamb for our sakes!

V

Of course, that means we've been recast: as liberated royalty. We can leave the Egyptian scene behind. We've now got a regal part to share in the script of God's reign! Remember the anti-racist lunch counter sit-ins of the early 1960s? No doubt those folks found it hard to stay seated at the counter. Dime-store thugs burned their arms with cigarettes. They poured sugar on these diners' heads while calling them names that had been ringing in their ears since the days of slavery. Yet those lunch counter activists might as well have been seated at a lavish banquet. For they held themselves like royalty—backs straight, sitting proud at a lunch counter deemed for whites only. Through every affliction the sit-in participants held their heads high. Perhaps they could see Egypt beginning to fall behind them, and ahead of them a kind of coronation. Call it: keeping your eyes on the prize. Could it be that they knew the Lamb had been slain to bring on God's royal finale? That it was time for them to assume a new role, too: as kings, queens, even priests for God's new reign? Of course, their royal exodus from Egypt may open up some problems for comfortable folks like us. We mainliners, after all, are more dazzled by Egyptian blandishments: investment portfolios, travel allowances, or pension plans. Those fleshpots of Egypt don't look bad, especially when you're white or middle class. Truth is, some folks may find it easier to bolt from Egypt than we do. It seems we all have quite a few shares in Pharaoh's stock exchange. Yet the role of liberated royalty may still be open to us, too—if we can let go of our pretensions long enough to enter into the part. Maybe we too can begin leaving Egypt behind with a kind of childlike glee.

In a little town in South Dakota the local church Christmas pageant had begun to lose its luster. There were many more kids than there were sparkling angel costumes. The cast was in chaos until a resolution to this knotty problem could be found. Then someone hit upon the idea: Why just one Mary, one Joseph, when every child can play the part? The night of the performance the audience was abuzz. When the music sounded, a stream of Marys processed down one side while a gaggle of Josephs sauntered down the other—all meeting at a high-traffic manger scene around a helpless little baby. Oh, the children weren't clad in dazzling raiment, just bathrobes or sheets. Yet each child strolled in like royalty—head held high. The good news is this: thanks to the Lamb, we too have received a regal part in God's Passover plot! Imagine that, folks like us cast as kings, queens, even priests in God's liberation script. Good news! The wounded Lamb has given us a royal part in God's new reign.

So here we are: a knock-kneed cast with a whole new script. Our new liberation role won't be easy to perform. But we can count on the Lamb's Passover plot to provide for a royal finale of freedom. Therefore let's play our part with gospel abandon. After all, Christ is always there to give a hand. So "Lights, camera, . . . " There, you said it: "Action!"

Sermon 3

Homiletical Rationale

In chapter 6 we learned what the rhetoric of Romans 8:18–30 was trying to *do*. This text wants hearers to consider suffering and glory as of a piece. How? When creation and believers groan, it is more than the interminable suffering we expect, it is also the work of the Spirit. The text is not interested in top-down spirituality of escapism or pietism. Rather, the rhetoric intends a bottom-up movement that locates the Spirit, the pledge of the apocalyptic turning of the ages, not just in our little, speechless, prayerful "hearts," but in the birthing of a new creation. The sermon, therefore, tries to move toward such an understanding. The introduction raises the issue of the Holy Spirit as a vague presence in our rough-and-tumble lives. By the end of the sermon, hearers realize that the Spirit is there not to escape from suffering and the world, but for engaging it in its transformation.

Since there was no apocalyptic form in Romans 8:18–30, our genre analysis coalesced with our symbol analysis. Thus both the route of our sermon and its "signs," or way of interpreting our world, will focus on the figure of the "woman in travail." The route is suggested by the figure itself and the forms it is typically found in. In most Hebrew Bible forms, the woman in travail indicates the presence of pain, suffering, and usually inescapable judgment. In apocalyptic texts, however, and especially in Romans 8, the figure points to pain toward an imminent birth of something new. Our sermon will therefore follow a similar generic "route." Symbolically, images of suffering and birth will underlie the sermon as a witness to its own way of "preaching in the new creation."

Sermon Text: Romans 8:18–30 (Day of Pentecost B)

Title: We've Got Spirit

There's an old saying we all know from our youth. It goes something like this: "Two's company; three's a crowd." Apparently, we don't always know what to do with the third person, the fifth wheel, or the sixth player on a basketball team. "Two's company," we say, "three's a crowd." Well it seems we Christians have the same problem with the Spirit. Sure there's God and, well, you can't do without Christ. But just what good is the Holy Spirit? With everything else we have to worry about in our rough-and-tumble world, just what do you do with the "Spirit"?

I

Of course, in a way we Christians *live* in the Spirit. The Holy Spirit is the air we breathe. Day in, day out, we church folk dwell in Holy Spirit. It all starts with baptism. Whether cooing baby decked out in white lace or knock-kneed adult in Sunday best, our baptismal procedure's the same!

134

We splash a little water around. Then we lay wet hands on a moist head and say: "You've got Spirit!" Now of course we're not always sure. Sometimes we consider Holy Spirit an extra gift, a sign of special blessedness— a tingle of the spine for those who've grown in the faith. Kind of like antilock brakes and a rear-window defogger on a new car. They're important, but not standard equipment for every new model. But then we remember that the Spirit is always the Spirit of Christ. With Christ, we don't need to shop for Spirit like options on a new car. Christ is Grace incarnate. So for us, Spirit is *God's* gift, too. God showers Spirit on us at baptism, and the gift stays good for life. God lavishes the Spirit upon us and invites us to live lavishly in it. Consider for a moment what we do every Sunday morning. Think about all the times we celebrate life in the Spirit just during worship! We invoke the Spirit's presence in prayer. Then, before even cracking open the Bible, we ask the Holy Spirit to illumine our reading of the Word. After the sermon we rise to our feet to confess our belief in the Spirit. Then, as if that weren't enough, we send each other on our way with a blessing for the fellowship of the Spirit. Our worship just tells it like it is. We Christians dwell in the Spirit. The Holy Spirit surrounds our life together. We live in the Spirit.

II

But let's get real: we also live in a world groaning for relief. We inhabit a creation sighing for an end to the pain. We Spirit-dwelling church folk also live in a world longing for release. We see it every time we turn on the TV news. Just look at the strains on our worldly home. On one channel there's a Bosnian woman wailing at the edge of a crater in a Sarajevo city park. An artillery barrage has just taken her child. The scarred landscape of the park, the charred trees, and the pain of a whole people seem to cry out through the woman's voice: "Lord, how long?" Now change the channel. Tune in to the news about the latest oil spill. Fish float on blackened water with mouths still moving. Helpless sea gulls with oil-soaked wings lie squawking on a beach. Even the playful sea lions, coated in petrochemical goo, are yelping for the camera. On our TVs the sea creatures seem to cry as with a single voice: "Lord, how long?" Now turn to the local news broadcast. The story is still the same. Some farmers in the next county are under financial pressure to produce. So they overtilled the land. Now a picture shows the farmers' topsoil drifted in a ditch. Suddenly the wind strews the bone-dry dust against a hazy sunset. As you listen to the report, you hear the dust-laden wind howling creation's sigh: "How long, Lord?" Surely we know: our world desires an end to suffering. We live in a world groaning for relief.

III

No wonder we church folk sigh for redemption, too. We Christians cry out for an end to suffering. We, too, groan for release. Dwelling in the Spirit offers no exemption from the world's pain. You know the score. There you are: a worker at a chemical plant slumped in a chair in the doctor's office. Diagnosis: cancer. But with a lump in your throat it takes all your strength just to moan, "Oh, God." Or maybe you're a logger who loses a job because currency troubles have made commodities like lumber too pricey. You carry your last paycheck from the sawmill home to your spouse and children. But you don't greet them; you just keep sobbing, "Oh, God!" Or perhaps the new world economy has only forced you to spend all your time at work for fear of being the next person downsized. On the rare occasion when you're home early enough for supper, you look across the dinner table only to see strangers in the other chairs. And all you can mutter with your face in your hands is: "Oh, my God." Well, no wonder we spend time every Sunday praying for ourselves and for the world. Our longing is one and the same. We pray for the rancorous family two pews ahead. And we pray for the woman dying in the nursing home down the street. And we even pray for the starving masses half way 'round the globe. Then, at the end of the prayer, with an almost imperceptible sound, we groan, "Amen." It seems we also sigh for redemption. We church folk share in crying for an end to the suffering. Truth is—we groan too.

IV

But listen closely: we do not sigh alone. We sigh with the Holy Spirit. When we groan, the Spirit groans with us. Our prayers are accompanied by Holy Spirit. Now let's be clear. We're not talking about the Spirit rubber-stamping our prayers. We don't need Holy Spirit for that—just some divine lackey. We say something different. When we groan with creation, longing for release, it is actually the Spirit praying through us. Well, imagine that! We fancy ourselves alone talking to God, presenting petitions like motions at a meeting. But before we even get a word in edgewise, the Spirit is already praying God's redemptive will through us. No wonder the old spiritual goes: "Every time I feel the Spirit moving in my heart, I will pray!" Our groaning prayers are not for goading the Spirit, but for responding to the Spirit among us. Of course, that turns everything upside down. We assume our world needs a dose of Spirit from the top down for things to turn out right. Well, surprise! In our groaning, Spirit is already bubbling up from below. After all, what else should the Spirit of God be doing than strengthening us in our weakness? So listen closely, people of God: when we groan, the Spirit groans with us. We do not sigh alone. The Spirit sighs with us.

V

Well, that's just what we need! The Spirit is there to strengthen us during our travail. We get comfort from the Spirit to get through the pain to new birth. You see, God doesn't give us the Spirit to make us comfortable in the electric blanket sense. The goal of the Holy Spirit's groaning is not to keep us satisfied with the status quo. Hardly! The Spirit does not make comfortable; the Spirit comforts. No wonder the coming of the new creation is compared to birth pangs. Sure there is pain. Yet there is also hope—for a new world is coming to birth. So the Spirit comforts us, *strengthens* us, as God's new creation is born. With each contraction the pain intensifies. Yet with each Spirit breath the joy of new birth comes closer. Can you see it? Already a new creation is crowning. And the Spirit is groaning to help. We all remember the news reports a few summers ago about the carnage in Rwanda. The Hutu and Tutsi tribes there were at each other's throats in a Rwandan civil war. At first, one tribe committed most of the carnage. Before long, the other tribe struck back and had the first tribe's ragtag army on the run. In the meantime, all the Rwandan people suffered. Many died from vicious machete attacks. Others collapsed on the way to refugee camps. Still others languished in exile as the world looked on helplessly. Yet one woman refused to give in. In the midst of her people's pain, she went into labor to give birth to a baby girl: a small newborn swaddled amid clashing tribes and mayhem. Yet with all the old battles over allegiances and identities swirling about her, do you know the name her mother gave the baby? Her mother called her Esperance. Her name means "Hope." Her mother named her hope. Well this is why God's Spirit has come to our aid, too: to comfort us as the new age is born among us. God's Spirit is here to give hope through the birth pangs—to new creation!

So imagine that. The Spirit is not some fifth wheel, or a cheap comfort for numbing the pain of the world. Hardly. God gives us Spirit until new creation comes to birth. So take heart! These troubles are actually birth pangs. And we are not alone. We've got Spirit.

Index of Scripture

Index of Authors